# The Children You Gave Us

### A HISTORY OF 150 YEARS OF SERVICE TO CHILDREN

# The Children You Gave Us

## A HISTORY OF 150 YEARS OF SERVICE TO CHILDREN

By
Jacqueline Bernard
With a Memoir by Art Buchwald
and
Foreword by Joseph L. Reid
Child Welfare League of America

Jewish Child Care Association of New York
1973

OTHER BOOKS BY JACQUELINE BERNARD

Journey Toward Freedom: The Story of Sojourner Truth
**W. W.** Norton, 1967

Voices From The Southwest
Scholastic Publishers, 1972

Bloch Publishing Company, New York, N. Y., Distributor

Copyright © 1972 Jewish Child Care Association of New York
Library of Congress Catalog Card Number: 72-87122
SBN-0-8197-0356-7
Printed in the United States of America

To the men and women, a small and committed group in each generation, who came forward to meet the needs of the bereft children — the orphaned, the destitute, the neglected — of New York's Jewish community for the past century and a half, this book is dedicated. Many are named in these pages. Many more are not, because the roster is a long one; in some cases, time has erased the names. To these compassionate people — voluntary leaders and staff members — who struggled to meet the desperate need of their brothers and the children of their brothers in a time of widespread poverty, and to serve the children better as knowledge and resources grew, this story is dedicated. This record of their successes and failures, of what they brought to the lives not only of the 70,000 children they cared for — but to the manyfold more they helped to grow up at home — is a moving chapter in the biography of the family of man.

# ACKNOWLEDGMENTS

This history of the Jewish Child Care Association was made possible by the many alumni, former staff, trustees, friends—and present staff too numerous to mention—who gave so generously of their time to help the writer in her research. In particular, I wish to thank Maurice Bernstein, Julia Goldman, Dr. Maurice Hexter, Aaron L. Jacoby, Lucille Lazar, Sally Melnick, Elizabeth Radinsky, Esther Simon, Evelyn Spiegel and Sarah Sussman for helping bring to life aspects of this history to which they personally contributed.

My thanks, too, to Hy Bogen, Sara Egelson, David Farber, Nathan Loewenstein, Eve Rabinowitz, Chester Rohrlich, Al Rudick, Lillian Schwartz, Murray Sprung, Katherine Stroock, and Lilly Turitz. And, for helping me pursue special trails, thanks are due Herschel Alt, John Greenburgh, Joan Lewisohn Simon, and Philip Soskis.

The librarians of the American Jewish Historical Society in Waltham, the Jewish Collection of the New York Public Library, the Columbia University School of Social Work, and the Wurzweiler School of Social Work of Yeshiva University helped obtain essential materials. Leah Gudes and Estelle Plung of the JCCA library contributed an enthusiastic interest and tireless patience that made it a pleasure to turn to them, as I did almost daily.

Finally my thanks to Donald L. Newborg whose suggestions were invaluable. And to Helene Weintraub whose idea it was to produce a 150th anniversary history. Without her support, criticism, and hours of collaborative effort, the work never would have been realized.

Jacqueline Bernard
*New York, September, 1972*

# CONTENTS

**COVER PHOTO:**

Children on Way to Kindergarten—*Hebrew Sheltering Guardian Society Orphanage*—1902

# PREFACE

"The principle of *tikkun olam* — the responsibility of
every person to make the world a better place — is
evident through the services and programs JCCA
provides to children and families in need."
*Vice President Joseph R. Biden, Jr.*
*Washington, D.C., April 24, 2012*

In the past 40 years since *The Children You Gave Us* was
published, Jewish Child Care Association has continued to be a
leader, an innovator, and a pioneer in addressing the changing
needs of New York City's most vulnerable children and families,
while maintaining our high quality of service.

JCCA has responded to the needs of a new wave of immigrants from the former Soviet Union, pioneered techniques to
assess the quality of our programs, and created new and effective
foster care initiatives. Our comprehensive services — including
early childhood initiatives, mental health and preventive services,
residential treatment, adoption, foster care, education support, and
services in the Jewish community — help 16,000 children and
families of all faiths and backgrounds each year. JCCA is one
of the oldest and most respected multicultural child and family
service agencies in the country.

We are thrilled that this new printing of *The Children You
Gave Us* allows us to share some of our most significant ac-
complishments of the past four decades in Jewish Child Care
Association's history. Below are a few highlights:

1978    Pleasantville Diagnostic Center is founded to provide
        intensive diagnostic evaluations for boys.

1984    A new Child Care Center opens in Forest Hills, serving
        many children from immigrant families.

        JCCA opens its first outpatient Mental Health and Pre-
        ventive Services program.

| 1989 | JCCA is one of the first agencies to be awarded a contract to provide Children's Intensive Case Management services from the New York State Office of Mental Health. |
|------|---|
| 1994 | JCCA launches a new project to serve the special needs of Jewish high school and college-age students with autism spectrum disorders and/or learning disabilities. |
| 1995 | JCCA holds its first symposium on adoption. |
| 1999 | JCCA opens the Bukharian Teen Lounge, a safe haven for immigrant high school students from the Central Asian part of the former Soviet Union, offering them support and guidance on living in a new country while retaining their traditional heritage. |
| 2000-08 | For each year since the inception of the City's annual performance review, JCCA's Foster Boarding Home programs are rated "Excellent." |
| 2002 | JCCA's Foster Boarding Home programs become community-based with offices in the South Bronx and central Brooklyn. |
| 2006 | JCCA begins the Partners in Caring program for Bukharian families in Queens and launches Journey, a program providing mental health treatment alternatives to incarceration for youth. |
| 2007 | JCCA's Preventive Services program is one of five in Brooklyn selected to implement Improved Outcomes for Children (IOC), a program of NYC's Children's Services (formerly ACS). |
| 2008 | JCCA is one of six agencies in the state awarded the innovative Bridges to Health (B2H) program. |
| 2009 | JCCA opens Brooklyn Democracy Academy, a transfer school in partnership with the Department of Education.

JCCA opens the Pursuing Our INdependence Together (POINT) Independent Living Program for young adults with special needs in partnership with Westchester Jewish Community Services.

JCCA also opens Gateways, a specialized program for sexually exploited and trafficked girls. |

JCCA opens the Kew Gardens Hills Youth Center, a preventive afterschool program for Orthodox Jewish male teens who live and attend yeshivas and other schools in the central Queens neighborhood.

2010    JCCA purchases a larger permanent home for the Bukharian Teen Lounge, its afterschool program for Bukharian youth in the Queens community.

2011    JCCA opens a new headquarters for our Brooklyn programs: Mental Health and Preventive Services, Foster Home Services, and Bridges to Health.

2012    JCCA celebrates 100 years of pioneering cottage-style residential living on its Westchester Campus.

As we approach our 200th anniversary in 2022, we will continue to meet new challenges and embrace new opportunities, yet our commitment to New York's children and families will remain the same. We will continue to provide leadership, innovative clinical approaches, a commitment to excellence, and compassion to all our clients — for every child deserves to grow up hopeful.

*Richard Altman*
*Chief Executive Officer, JCCA*
*April 2013*

# FOREWORD

"THE CHILDREN YOU GAVE US" is one of the first full-scale historical portraits of a major American child welfare agency. It is an appropriate first, for the Jewish Child Care Association of New York and its ancestor agencies have often been innovators and forerunners in the child welfare field. Its history, a fascinating one, reveals patterns of development which are almost identical with the history of child welfare services in the United States. Today, heir to virtually all of the city's Jewish orphanages (which long ago closed their doors to offer more individualized ways of care), the Association is one of the largest and most diversified voluntary child welfare agencies in the country.

It is easy to forget how radically attitudes toward children have changed in these United States. The description of the treatment of children in the first stages of the agency's history in the 19th Century seems incredible unless one knows something of the prevalent public attitudes of that era.

In 1860 when New York's first Jewish orphanage (later to be known as the Hebrew Orphan Asylum) opened, dependent children were often housed in public alms houses—dumping grounds for every form of adult pauper, from the mentally deranged or retarded to the physically handicapped. Thousands of other children were "cared for" through the notorious "vendue system". Under that system, dependent children, as well as pauper adults, were put on an auction block and whoever offered to care for them at the lowest price got the contract for their care. It was also a time when the public did not object to children as young as seven working ten to twelve hours a day, six days a week, in factories and cotton mills.

Many today raise questions about the place of the voluntary agency, and of the sectarian agency in particular. To read this history is to understand the vital importance of the volunteer citizen's role in protecting children, and the value of widespread volunteer participation in the policy-making of child welfare. Each decade brought new problems—massive waves of immigration, wars and depressions. The community leaders who headed New York's Jewish orphanages and children's agencies were severely challenged by change, the most difficult challenge of all. They met that challenge in remarkable ways.

i

The achievements of the JCCA are numerous: The development of one of the first cottage plan institutions in the United States; the creation of the first child guidance clinic within a children's institution; the development of foster family care; the widow's subsidy for child care; the development of specialized education for emotionally disturbed children; the development of the small group residence as an alternative form of placement, particularly for teenagers; recognition of the role of foster parents as early as 1919 (setting the stage for today's foster parents associations); and many others.

In our own time, the Jewish Child Care Association has met with imagination and strong social responsibility the challenge of the passing of the traditional orphan. Its administrators and board members have helped its supporting public—both private and governmental—to understand the need for increasingly complex and costly programs to serve the very troubled children and families of today, and to reach out to others as yet unserved. While many other child care agencies and institutions drifted into uselessness because they could not face change, this organization has responded positively to the challenges of changing social needs and developing psychological insight. It can be fairly said that no other agency in the United States can claim a greater list of progressive experiments and innovations to serve children.

The history of the organization provides a fine example of partnership between government and private philanthropy. Almost from its beginning, the State and City of New York helped to finance the JCCA because they believed that it was performing a public task. But the JCCA leadership was never content simply to spend what government gave them. The fundamental commitment of the Jewish community to charity and to the concept of the equality of men meant that the agency felt impelled to strive for excellence—seeking to provide for the children in its charge care equal to that which each member of the Jewish community would want for his own child. This sense of communal commitment is unmatched by any other group in the country. It helps to account for the fact that Jewish child welfare agencies in general usually rank at the top in excellence, innovation, and in willingness to change to meet current needs.

Though presently threatened throughout the country, it is clear from this vivid record that the voluntary agency with the courage and the sensitivity to reach out to meet the needs of its time is an essential institution in American life and must be preserved.

Professionals and laymen in the child welfare field are all too conscious of the deficiencies of today's child welfare programs. They are keenly aware of present inadequacies and failures. However, they can find hope for the future in this remarkable history, for it is a history of how the sensitive responsiveness of the Jewish community to the needs of children resulted, as understanding increased, in a rapid evolution of sound child care practices.

Perhaps the greatest challenge that the future offers is how to ensure that all our children in every community, regardless of race or religion, may receive services of equally high quality. For, as long as a high percentage of children requiring child welfare services receive care of indifferent quality, and as long as many children receive no services at all because their problems are thought to be too complicated and too costly to remedy, all high quality services are endangered. And, more significantly, if we ignore the lessons of history and the knowledge within our grasp, we fail the legions of children who need humane and sensitive help, we imperil our most valuable resource, and we endanger our future as a nation.

*Joseph H. Reid, Executive Director*
*Child Welfare League of America*

# REMINISCENCES

(At Sesquicentennial Brunch of Jewish Child Care Association of New York)

I seem to be a man who is constantly fulfilling his childhood dreams of glory. Somewhere back in the dim past as a foster child of 10 years old, I dreamed that someday I would be the guest of honor at just such an affair. I didn't know the event would take place at the Pierre Hotel — obviously I had never heard of a Pierre Hotel — but in my fantasy I saw myself on a podium such as this talking about the struggles of my childhood and how I overcame them. I particularly liked the part in my dreams when I gave myself a standing ovation.

There has been a great deal of confusion as to where I fit in the Jewish Child Care picture, so I would like to clear it up today. I was placed in the Hebrew Orphan Asylum when I was six years old. The H.O.A., which was then located on Amsterdam Avenue, for all its glory did not look exactly like the Fontainebleau. The architecture, if my memory serves me right, was early Sing Sing.

But I didn't stay long in the Home. After they checked my health and issued me the uniform of the day, it was decided that I would make a *swell* foster child. So after about six weeks of quarantine a couple named Morris from Hollis, Long Island came to the H.O.A. and took my three sisters and me into their home.

The status of a foster child, particularly *for* the foster child, is a strange one. He's part of no man's land.

If you lived at the H.O.A. you had the security of numbers. There were hundreds in the same boat as you were and that in itself gave you some sense of belonging. A foster home, on the other hand, is something else again. The child knows instinctively that there is nothing permanent about the setup, and he is, so to speak, on loan to the family he is residing with. If it doesn't work out, he can be swooped up and put in another home.

It's pretty hard to ask a child or a foster parent to make a large emotional commitment under these conditions, and so I think I was about seven years old, when confused, lonely and terribly insecure I said to myself, "The hell with it. I think I'll become a humorist."

From then on I turned everything into a joke. Starting as the class clown, I graduated to making fun of all authority figures from the principal of the school to the social service worker who visited every month. When a person is grown up and he attacks authority, society pays him large sums of money. But when he's a kid and he makes fun of authority, they beat his brains in.

Having chosen this dangerous pastime of getting attention by poking fun at everything, I found I could survive. I had my bag of laughs, and I had my fantasies, which I must say were really great. Would you believe that I dreamed I was really the son of a Rothschild, and I was kidnapped by gypsies when I was six months old, and sold to a couple who were going to America?

If you believe that, would you believe the Rothschilds had hired France's foremost detective to find me and that it was only a matter of time when he would trace me to the foster home in Hollis, Long Island, and would you believe that once my true identity had been established, I would prevail on my Rothschild father to drop all charges against the people that had kidnapped me, and give them a substantial pension?

That's the kind of kid my social worker had to deal with.

I lived in three different foster homes during my 11-year association with the H.O.A. I never went to the orphan asylum itself except to get issued clothes or have my teeth fixed. I never had anything to do with the H.O.A. kids, except in the summer when I was sent to Camp Wakitan in Bear Mountain. The kids who lived in the H.O.A. didn't have too much use for those of us who came from foster homes — and so at camp my nose used to bleed a lot.

To add to my woes, two kids in Hollis who lived on my street went to the Methodist Camp located right next to Camp Wakitan. They didn't know I was a foster child, and I lived in deathly fear that they would discover I came from an orphanage. So I spent half my summers ducking behind trees, and hiding in the bottom of canoes, so my terrible secret wouldn't be found out.

I don't wish to give the impression that I was unhappy in my role as a foster child. The people I lived with were kind to me and I had the benefit of a home life.

I never lost touch with my father and my three sisters and I are closer than many families who had their own homes from the start.

I guess if I look back on it I owe a great debt to the H.O.A. and to the people who really cared what happened to the Jewish children of New York.

I won't give you all the credit though. I owe some of it to World War II. The war came just at the right time for me, and at sixteen and a half, I ran away and joined the U. S. Marine Corps. The Marines turned out to be the finishing school for anything I hadn't learned as a foster child, and my big fantasy in the Marine Corps was to go back to Camp Wakitan and beat the hell out of all the kids from the H.O.A. who used to beat the hell out of me.

After the Marine Corps I went to the University of Southern California then to Paris in 1948.

In Paris I decided to make up for my deprived childhood by becoming the food and wine expert of the Paris Edition of the Herald Tribune. I lived it up with the International Set, sailed on Onassis' yacht, played roulette with King Farouk, and danced until dawn with the Duchess of Windsor.

I'd like to thank you all for helping to fulfill another one of my fantasies. I feel I have had a unique experience with few regrets. Every once in a while someone asks me, "How do you become a humorist?" I always reply, "Well first you have to become a foster child — and after that it all comes naturally."

Art Buchwald<br>
April, 1972

# GLOSSARY OF ABBREVIATIONS

| | |
|---|---|
| BHOA | Brooklyn Hebrew Orphan Asylum |
| HBS | Hebrew Benevolent Society |
| H-H | Hartman-Homecrest (a merger of Gustave Hartman Home and the Hebrew National Orphan Home) |
| HHI | Home for Hebrew Infants |
| HNOH | Hebrew National Orphan Home |
| HOA | Hebrew Orphan Asylum |
| HSGS | Hebrew Sheltering Guardian Society |
| IOA | Israel Orphan Asylum (later Gustave Hartman Home for Children) |
| JCCA | Jewish Child Care Association of New York |
| JCCB | Jewish Children's Clearing Bureau |
| JYSB | Jewish Youth Services of Brooklyn |

# Chapter 1

# "By Their Own Nation"

*"These people may travel and trade to and in New Netherland and live and remain there, provided the poor among them shall not become a burden to the company or to the community, but be supported by their own nation."* AMSTERDAM CHAMBER OF THE WEST INDIA COMPANY IN LETTER TO GOVERNOR STUYVESANT, APRIL 26, 1655.

I N 1822, when the Hebrew Benevolent Society was founded, New York was a bustling port, prospering in the explosion of foreign trade that followed the war of 1812. But, by today's standards, it was still a very small city.

Maps of the day show the blocks laid out only as far north as 13th Street and the northern wards generously sprinkled with cornfields and pastures. Brooklyn, a ferry's ride away, had recently been designated a "village." The very nation was new. In March, its citizens celebrated the second inauguration of their fifth president, James Monroe.

It was in this setting that a group of American-born English and Dutch Jews met in Lower Manhattan, on April 8, to decide what to do with $300.

Tradition has it that the sum was the unspent balance of a collection hastily taken up, two years earlier, to help a critically ill Jewish veteran of the War of Independence. But the old man's name is lost. Perhaps it was never recorded, although that would seem strange. There were few Revolutionary soldiers among the Jews and they were greatly honored. For reasons of delicacy, however, recipients of Jewish charity frequently were identified — if at all — only by their initials.

The story goes that the sick old man was discovered lying in a city hospital by John J. Hart, Joseph Davies and other members of what was then New York's only congregation — Shearith Israel. Penniless and alone, he clearly needed help. No hospitalized Jew could expect to keep the dietary laws without friends to intervene. And there were unpleasant stories of Hebrews on their death beds being pressured to convert to Christianity. With 20 different and equally determined groups angling for the souls of the city's Jews, such stories were easy to credit.

Despite the best efforts of his new friends, the old man had died, leaving them with the left-over fund. The use of charitable money was not to be treated lightly by Jews in New York, in 1822. Once very simple, the problem was becoming complex.

It was 167 years since the first group of Portuguese Jews had landed on the shore of what was then New Amsterdam and been given permission to stay, but only on condition that they always take care of their own poor.

Over the years, the Jewish community had faithfully adhered to its bargain, mainly through the systematic efforts of Shearith Israel. The congregation provided free burial, wood in winter, matzoth before Passover, and sometimes free medical care and interest-free loans for the poor. It even had a most unusual (for its period) system of pensions to protect its members in bad times. So long as every religious Jew living in New York was a member of one small congregation, the Shearith Israel program served the community well enough. Old people, and widows and their children could be provided for in their own homes. And penniless orphans, when necessary, could be boarded out at the expense of the congregation or apprenticed to a local tradesman.

But this deep sense of responsibility New York's Jews displayed toward their own was also part of an older obligation. Was it not written in the Old Testament: "He who sustains God's creatures is as though he had created them"? Wherever Jews worshipped, the rabbi taught three things: to study the Torah, to pray, and to pursue acts of kindness toward the less fortunate. That third practice — *Tzedakah,* the charity which also means justice — was basic to a meritorious life. In the new environment, it was further reinforced by the ideals of justice and democracy imbedded in the American Revolution.

And in New York there was still a third reason for a Jew to help his co-religionists. The busy, tolerant city had no ghetto walls or discriminatory laws to push the Jewish community together, whereas it produced many seductive business, social and cultural pressures. The lazy and the ambitious alike daily were tempted to forget their origins and ignore such obstacles to easy assimilation as the Sabbath and the dietary laws.

The congregation's social services helped combat this and keep Jews within the fold by reinforcing the influence of the synagogue. But by 1822 that influence was weakening. The Jewish population was growing too large. There were disputes within the congregation between the "Ancient Hebrew Families" — the earlier Sephardic arrivals — and the more recent Ashkenazim immigrants. And what a shock, the preceding year, to learn that a Jewish woman actually had died in the poor house! *Despite* the fact that a specially appointed committee of the congregation had clearly stated that the "first duty" of every trustee was to make certain *no* Jew *ever* went to the poor house.

For years, Jewish immigration from Western Europe to the United States had come in intermittent drops. But the turbulence that had followed the Napoleonic Wars had swelled the drops to a steady trickle. True there still were only 500 Jews in a total city population of 123,706. But 500 represented an increase of almost 43% in only 28 years.

No longer was every residence within easy walking distance of Shearith Israel. Most Jews did continue to make their homes on Pearl, Water, and lower Greenwich Streets, close to the Mill Street synagogue. But an increasing number were moving into new homes "uptown", which was to say north of Canal Street but still well below the former potters field that soon would become Washington Square.

How much longer could a single synagogue shoulder responsibility for the fast-spreading community?

The group of men assembled in Manhattan, that April day in 1822, clearly felt the time had come to supplement in some organized way the charitable efforts of their congregation. They founded the city's first general Jewish charitable society independent of the synagogue and called it the Hebrew Benevolent Society. Daniel Jackson was elected the first president. And the old veteran's leftover $300 provided a treasury. One month later the *New York Mercantile Advertiser* published the following "communication":

*Charitable Institution* — A society under the name of the "Hebrew Benevolent Society of the City of New York" has been formed, and Mr. Daniel Jackson has been chosen president, and Mr. Joseph Jackson, treasurer. The object of the society is to ameliorate the condition of the unfortunate of the same faith, whether residents or non-residents of the city. We are happy to find that the members of the house of "Israel" inhabiting this free country, and enjoying all the blessings of civil and religious liberty, are alive to the finest feelings of humanity, in founding an institution which reflects honor on the projectors. Native citizens, who feel an interest in the improvement of the condition of this too much neglected portion of the human family, are invited to aid in the support of the funds of the society.

The society was incorporated under Chapter 14 of New York State Laws of 1832 by a special act of the New York State legislature, introduced February 2, 1832, by Mordecai Myers. Myers was one of the earliest Jewish representatives in the New York State Assembly and the great-great-grandfather of the contemporary American poet, Robert Lowell. Point 3 of the act stated the society's objectives to be "charitable and to afford relief to its members in case of sickness and infirmity."

This earliest formal statement of the purposes of the first incorporated ancestor of the Jewish Child Care Association of New York makes no specific mention of children. Their needs could still be met in the traditional ways mentioned earlier. More numerous, the Catholics and Protestants already were finding it necessary to build special institutions for their orphaned or destitute young — to save them from the public almshouse and the daily experience of "the raving of the maniac, the frightful contortions of the epileptic, the driveling and senseless sputtering of the idiot, the garrulous temper of the decrepit, neglected old age, the peevishness of the infirm, the accumulated filth of all these . . ."

There was a growing feeling on the part of many that children needed better care than that. The New York Society for the Relief of Poor Widows with Small Children had been organized in 1797 by Isabella Graham and, in 1806, had opened its first small home for 12 "homeless, full orphan children." New York's Roman

Catholics also had opened an asylum. By 1818, it was caring for 28 children.

Even without the burden of an institution, however, the resources of the new Benevolent Society often were strained to the breaking point by periodic disasters. Only three months after the HBS's founding, an epidemic of yellow fever swept the city. It was a chronic problem, bred by the filthy streets described in so many chronicles. Ten years later, cholera broke out. Nearly half the city's population of one-quarter million fled to Connecticut and Long Island. But the poorest had no means of travel.

Such calamities left their toll of Jewish widows and orphans and other victims to be helped by Shearith Israel and the Hebrew Benevolent Society. The calamities also helped keep down the population. Nevertheless, by 1840, the increasing flow of immigration — largely now from Germany and Poland — had hoisted the Jewish census to 7,000. One-half of New York's Jews were German by then. One-third were Polish. The community was less united. Synagogues were multiplying, and the need for strong Jewish philanthropic institutions outside the synagogues was no longer in question. In the 1840's, with Mordecai Manuel Noah as its president, the Hebrew Benevolent Society moved to fill the breach.

Noah was a man of his time. Grand Sachem of Tammany Hall — which only then was becoming a powerful political machine — he also, at various times, was Sheriff of New York, American consul to Tangiers, and a pioneer in the movement to set up a Jewish state in Palestine.

As the first eminent Jewish figure in New York journalism, Noah founded, edited, and published, between 1820 and 1840, seven different dailies. At one time, James Gordon Bennett worked on Noah's *Enquirer,* and, legend would have it, founded the *Herald* — ancestor of the later *Herald Tribune* — on $100 borrowed from his former employer.

During Noah's nine-year presidency, membership in the society soared, and the annual anniversary dinner became *the* social event of the year for the Jewish community. At first, non-Jewish political leaders considered it a duty to be present. Later they would not have missed it for anything.

Held in such fashionable halls as Niblo's Saloon or the Chinese Assembly Rooms, the dinners were free to the guests invited. But those present of course were expected to contribute generously during the after-dinner appeal. It was Noah who inaugurated at these dinners the presidential custom of wearing suspended by a ribbon from his neck a gold medallion designed by his wife. The back of the medallion — today in the possession of the Jewish Child Care Association of New York — shows a dove carrying a twig in its beak, an allusion to the biblical Noah.

These annual dinners — from which all women were excluded — lasted for hours. After the food, six to twelve formal toasts were regularly presented, each followed by an appropriate response prepared well in advance. First, a toast to the day itself. Second, to the American president. Next, to the city. And so forth — through charity, education, religion and religious liberty, our co-religionists, the clergy, the press, our sister societies. Now followed an unlimited number of improvised toasts and responses. The wines were always excellent, the evening progressively gayer.

Fortunately, the dinners also proved outstandingly successful fund-raising affairs and the membership rolls grew as fast as the demands of the growing Jewish community for charitable assistance.

In 1841, in the midst of a crippling economic crisis, the society helped only 195 individuals. During the next crisis, in 1858, it received more than ten times that number of appeals for assistance. And this despite the fact that the large German-Jewish population, ten years earlier, had organized a charitable society of its own. The German Hebrew Benevolent Society was "to assist the poor of the Hebrew faith and to erect a hospital to take care of the poor and sick . . ."

The presence of two such similar societies brought predictable problems. The German Benevolent Society aided only German Jews, but the Hebrew Benevolent aided all Jews. Their efforts frequently overlapped — a problem that would occur and re-occur in the next 100 years of Jewish philanthropic effort.

Strenuous attempts soon were initiated to get the two societies to pool their strengths. Even then, people seriously wondered if country of origin was *really* relevant when dealing with victims of distress and disaster. But pressures to unite were unavailing.

By 1850, the Jewish population had reached 16,000 — an increase of another 230% in only 10 years — and the need for a home for orphans had become acute.

Three years earlier, a former mayor, Philip Hone, had described the city's problem: "Our good city of New York has already arrived at the state . . . where the two extremes of costly luxury . . . and improvident waste are presented in daily and hourly contrast with squalid misery and hopeless destitution." As always the worst sufferers were the children.

Homeless urchins roamed the streets. Ragged little girls, newsboys, bootblacks, "canal boys", child beggars. Orphans sleeping in boxes or on stairways were a common sight. To the police all homeless children were the same — "street rats."

Who could be sure that no Jewish children were slipping through the loosening mesh of Jewish charities and ending up where so many other little vagrants did — among the brothels and beer halls of the notorious Five Points slum? With far smaller Jewish populations, New Orleans and Philadelphia already had Jewish orphanages. It was time that New York followed suit.

Led by Philip J. Joachimsen, a German-born lawyer who had succeeded Noah as president of the Hebrew Benevolent, and by the president of the German society — merchant and banker Joseph Seligman — the merger discussions went on and on. A merger of the two charitable societies was a necessary prerequisite to getting the support of a united community for the planned institution.

Meanwhile, funds for an orphanage were coming in. The seemingly inexhaustible estate of the New Orleans merchant, ship owner, real estate owner and philanthropist, Judah Touro, had included a $5,000 bequest for each of the two societies. The sum was about equal to the yearly expenditures of the Hebrew Benevolent. Now the minister of Reform Temple Emanu-El raised $8,000 more from the members of his congregation.

Still no merger. Needed was the firm psychological shove expertly applied in 1859 when Rabbi S. M. Isaacs published in his *Jewish Messenger* an alarming editorial. A Jewish child had been placed in a non-Jewish orphanage in New York and converted to Christianity!

This persuaded even the worst footdraggers to unite and elect the HBS president, Joachimsen, to head the merged groups. The *new* Hebrew Benevolent Society would continue its work among the poor. In addition, it was to found and maintain a home for orphans, and one for aged and indigent Jews. (A hospital — one of the original goals of the German Society — was no longer needed. The Jews Hospital — now Mount Sinai — had been founded in 1852 by members from Shearith Israel and Shaaray Tefillah led by Sampson Simson.)

The leather-bound *Minutes* of the new Hebrew Benevolent Society show no time was lost in appointing a committee to "repair to the two Five Points Missions" and rescue any Jewish children who might be found in those gospel-preaching institutions. President Joachimsen himself headed this vital task force.

In April, 1860, a three-story brick house with a basement was purchased for $10,500 at No. 1 Lamartine Place (now West 29th Street between 8th and 9th Avenues). Clearly too small for the anticipated need, it was to serve as a temporary asylum while a larger building was being constructed. The Society resolved to admit "Jewish orphans or half-orphans of this city from the ages of three to thirteen years." Orphans under three could be "maintained" by the Society until admissible. That meant they would be boarded out in the care of wet nurses — usually, in that day, Christian.

A supplementary act of incorporation passed by the state legislature, April 12, 1860, had vastly enlarged the HBS powers. The society now could "take, have, hold, and enjoy real and personal estate of the annual income of not exceeding $15,000." It could "take, and hold, and convey, and dispose of any real or personal property given, bequeathed or devised to them by deed, last will, and testament. . . ." It could sue in court for the recovery of subscriptions, dues, and voluntary donations. And the trustees were to have the "exclusive custody and control of the persons of such orphans, half-orphans, or indigent children of the age not exceeding 13 years as they may agree to maintain, provide for, educate, and instruct. . . ." They also could bind them out at 13 "to be taught and instructed in some necessary or useful employment, on such terms and restrictions, and to such persons, and upon such conditions, as the said Trustees may deem proper."

In the case of orphans, the legal guardian or nearest relative or one of the governors of the almshouse had to consent in writing to the society's assumption of responsibility. Half-orphans and indigent children also could be entrusted to the society by a guardian or relative. But if they were, instead, committed to its care by any "court, magistrate, or police justice" it was to be only "with the consent of said Trustees." The wary society preserved its right to say "no."

These powers were identical to those granted the New York Juvenile Asylum — today, Children's Village near Dobbs Ferry, New York — on its founding, seven years earlier, to care for the neglected and vagrant children of Irish and German immigrants. It had opened in a house on Bank Street with 57 children admitted the first day, and later that same year had moved to 55th Street with 200 charges. Altogether, in the course of its first year, it had admitted 1,000 children. But the New York Juvenile Asylum's articles of incorporation also had authorized the board of supervisors of the city and county of New York to support these children by paying the asylum a sum not exceeding $40 per year for each child committed. The sum was raised to $75 per capita in 1858, and again to $90 in 1863.

No such authorization was in the supplementary act of the Jewish society. The community still preferred to support its own, and, fortunately, its smaller numbers still permitted this.

Thirty children — including several rescued from the missions — soon were installed on Lamartine Place under the care of Superintendent Samuel E. Hart and his wife who served as matron. A group of women promptly organized a Ladies Sewing Society to keep the children in clothing and linen and also drew up firm rules and regulations for the Orphan's Home.

Life in that first small New York Jewish asylum continued quietly for a while, but always strictly regimented. Obedience and order were the rule, here as elsewhere in the child-caring institutions and proper families of the day. An orphanage ward had to develop a strong moral character to counteract the sea of chaos from which it so recently had been snatched.

Henry Bauer — "the first full orphan" and one of the first

seven boys to enter — in 1910 recalled the daily schedule as "get up, say your prayers, get your breakfast, go to school, come back, study your lessons, study Hebrew, get your supper, and go to bed. Very little play — very little play!"

And as for the food: "Mush and milk, and hominy and milk, and mush and molasses, and rice and milk — and in the evening we had milk and bread. We never had the taste of clear water, no, sir. I never could see the reason. We used to drink water on the sly out of the hydrants."

Every weekday morning, the superintendent, wearing a high hat and carrying a gold-headed cane, marched the boys and girls, two by two, to the public school. In the afternoon, he marched them back again.

The asylum had little living space. When not in school or sleeping the children appear to have been confined to a single room — the dining room. There were, of course, two of these — one for each sex. Each served as eating room, classroom, playroom and studyroom. It was before the days of plumbing. Architects were instructed, in 1862, to design two outside privies.

A few boys found such a life style unendurable, and absconded. But little Henry Bauer, despite the restrictions, seems to have been happy enough to stay where he was. He had been living with a Hebrew teacher on Second Street where he had "got more licking than grub," until a "fine old gentleman . . . noticed the time I was having, so he got me placed in the Home."

And the "Rules and Regulations of the Ladies Committee" inscribed in the *Minutes* suggest that the food was not quite as bad as he painted it. He correctly described the monotonous breakfast and supper. But dinner was *supposed* to be "either roast or stew with a vegetable" and, on Saturday, "in addition to their beef, fruit or pie."

The society lost no time starting its search for a lot on which to build a roomier institution. By February 14, 1861, it had obtained authorization from the State Assembly to erect a building for 200 children on 77th Street and Third Avenue on land donated by the City of New York. The state would contribute $35,000 toward the new asylum as soon as the society had spent $20,000 of its own money for the same purpose. Another $30,000 towards building costs would come from the city. The asylum would be "subject to the same regulation and visitation as other charitable institutions."

The campaign to raise the needed funds was led by Joseph Seligman, friend of Ulysses Grant and soon to be known as New York's leading Jewish banker. (He had become president on the resignation of Philip J. Joachimsen who now was organizing the 59th Volunteer New York Regiment and soon would lead it south to fight in the Civil War.)

Subscribers and donations were solicited on all sides. When Baron de Rothschild came to town an especially designated committee hastily called on him to request a contribution. The funds were raised, construction started, and, June 28, 1863, $725 more was appropriated "for the purpose of erecting outhouses" for the large child population anticipated. Young Henry Bauer held the Union flag high, November 5, 1863, as the new building was dedicated.

Four months before the move uptown, the orderly life of the orphans on Lamartine Place was rudely shattered by a sharp reminder of the war. An anti-draft mob rushed past their home to set fire to a neighboring house at which Horace Greeley sometimes stayed. The abolitionist editor of the *New York Tribune* was away, but the orphans watched wide-eyed as their superintendent helped the house's owners climb over a fence to the safety of a waiting carriage. Later police and militia in bloodstained white trousers were carried past their door.

"It was a very exciting time for the inmates," recalled the superintendent's son.

No harm came to the Jewish orphanage. The pogroms of New York City were aimed at Blacks, not Jews. A screaming mob headed for the huge Colored Orphan Asylum at 44th and Fifth Avenue, smashed the furniture and set the building on fire. Just in time the black children were ushered out the back and ferried to Blackwells Island — all but one terrified little girl who had hidden under a bed. She was pulled out and beaten to death by a crowd composed mainly of women.

Some months later the Lamartine Place home was sold for $10,250. Uptown, the children were already in the new building.

The first 52 had moved in late in 1863. Within a few years, the building — so proudly faced with the "best quality of brownstone" — already would be outgrown. The era of the great asylums had dawned for the Jewish orphans of New York.

# Chapter 2

# The Great Orphanages

*"We were a parcel of children, tied by a strange bond together."*
PETER SMITH, ALUMNUS, HEBREW SHELTERING GUARDIAN SOCIETY.

*"The HOA was for many years a mixture of oases of kindness and arid stretches of regimentation."* MAURICE BERNSTEIN, HOA ALUMNUS AND FORMER ADMINISTRATOR.

THE LAST HALF of the nineteenth century in America was a time of orphans—orphans and half-orphans and destitute children. In New York State alone, the Civil War left tens of thousands of such youngsters. From 1861 to 1866, the number in public almshouses increased from 8,000 to more than 26,000. The following year over 8,500 homeless children found temporary shelter in the Newsboys Lodging Houses of the Children's Aid Society.

By the end of the war, the 77th Street Orphan Home of the Hebrew Benevolent Society sheltered twice as many children as it had when it opened two years earlier.

Yet for a decade it did appear that one 200-bed orphanage might suffice the Jewish community. The war had interrupted the flow of immigration and the lull continued until the mid-seventies. Then the comfortable illusion shattered as the hopeful poor — many of them Jews — started pouring in once again from Europe. But instead of the Promised Land, the immigrants now encountered a prolonged depression — the worst the country had yet seen. Homeless children roamed the streets and alleys.

In 1870, the Hebrew Benevolent Society already had acknowledged the growing importance of its work with children by changing its name, and raising its dues from $5 to $25. By act of the state legislature, it had become the "Hebrew Benevolent and Orphan Asylum Society of the City of New York." Four years later, as the trustees eyed the rising immigrant tide, traditional

**13**

Jewish pride bent to the current institutional trend and a decision was made to seek public subsidies. For this, a further legislative act had to be obtained.

This granted the society the right to "enjoy the same benefits, and receive for the care, education, and maintenance (of its children) the like compensation now paid" the New York Juvenile Asylum. Compensation was $110 per child annually now, with an additional $13.50 per child for intra-mural education, should this be provided. That year, 1874, with a budget of $32,579.55, the Society received $23,203.97 — or about 70% — from the City.

The legislative act had come just in time. The following year, demands on institutions for dependent children in New York were further intensified when the state legislature passed Chapter 173, *Laws of 1875,* known as the "Children's Law." Long awaited, the law (with a strengthening amendment added in 1878) ordered the removal of all children over two from the almshouses. It further required that public authorities place impoverished youngsters at public expense in homes or institutions run by those of their parents' faith.

In the two decades that followed, this latter principle came under frequent attack. But at the Constitutional Convention of 1894, it was strongly defended by the convention's Committee on Charities, headed by HOA president Edward Lauterbach, and finally safely incorporated into Section 14, Article VIII of the new constitution.

Ironically, the leaders of the movement to save the children from the almshouses — a movement headed by Commissioner William Pryor Letchworth of the State Board of Charities — were fervent early proponents of family care rather than institutional care for children who could not live in their own homes. But the measure they urged — although the last child was not out of the almshouses until 1895 — brought an immediate boom to private children's institutions. In 1875, New York City had slightly more than 50 such institutions. Within five years, the number had doubled, with the new ones depending for their support largely on public funds.

But the influx of children to the Hebrew Orphan Asylum

(HOA) — as the orphanage of the Hebrew Benevolent Society came to be called — came not from the almshouse but from the renewed immigration.

Fortunately, by that time the former Benevolent Society was stripped for action and ready to concentrate on orphans. In 1873, just as a severe economic depression added new harshness to the immigrant dilemma, the HOA had joined with three other Jewish agencies to found the United Hebrew Charities. It transferred to the UHC its former relief-disbursing role and provided the new agency with a president, HOA vice-president Henry Rice. Over the next 34 years, the HOA would donate $647,100 to the new Hebrew Charities organization, which was the central relief-disbursing Jewish agency of the city.

Meanwhile the orphanage soon was filled to overflowing, and its Ladies Sewing Society rented an additional building at 234 East 86th Street to house the older girls and the youngest children. Faced with a continuing emergency, the board in 1878 made a firm decision: no more children from Brooklyn. (Brooklyn was then a separate city.)

Brooklyn Jews, who had been regular contributors to the HOA, were stunned that the Manhattan agency had so "summarily abandoned responsibility" for their children. They organized an emergency meeting at Temple Beth Elohim under the chairmanship of Sigismund Kaufman; and, with a cash capital of $2,000 and a membership of 300, invested $500 in renting a house large enough for 16 children at 384 McDonough Street, in what is now Bedford-Stuyvesant. As eight children moved in, a Ladies Sewing Society materialized and friendly neighbors began dropping by, bringing small contributions. Cakes, a basket of apples, six prayer books.

The state charter granted in August, 1878, gave the "Hebrew Orphan Asylum of the City of Brooklyn" (BHOA) the duty to house, educate and maintain the "Hebrew orphans" of Brooklyn until they could provide for themselves. In obedience to that charter, the institution for many years refused care to indigent children with two living parents.

Unfortunately, lopping off Brooklyn didn't resolve the problem in Manhattan. A second decision followed. From now on the HOA would take full advantage of the option provided in *its* charter. Some other means would have to be found for caring for the indigent children brought into court for "not having proper guardianship or visible means of existence." The institution had always had a certain reluctance to accept children through the courts. Now, with its space filled to 150% of capacity, it had ample excuse for selectivity.

Once again the Jewish community faced the old threat of Jewish children committed to non-Jewish institutions. And once again a public-spirited group headed by the former president of the Hebrew Benevolent Society, Philip J. Joachimsen, and his wife, Priscilla stepped into the breach.

Philip Joachimsen was throughout his life a remarkable public servant. An immigrant from East Germany at 14, he was assistant corporation counsel of New York City by 23 and later, as federal prosecutor, won fame for securing the first capital conviction against a slave trader. Disabled by a fall from his horse while leading his volunteer regiment during the Civil War, he was made a brigadier general by brevet order of the New York governor. By 1879, he was popularly known as "Judge" Joachimsen, having served from 1870-77 as a Judge of the Marine Court.

His wife was no less interesting. For a woman of her time, Priscilla Joachimsen had demonstrated remarkable public initiative. In 1870, she had helped found the Home for Aged and Infirm Hebrews, and for three years had served as its president. In 1878, she and her husband helped to found one of New York's first day care shelters for young children of destitute parents, the Ladies' Deborah Nursery. This nursery was unusual in having an all-woman board. Mrs. Joachimsen later resigned in a dispute over policies.

Now, in 1879, she became president of the new Hebrew Sheltering Guardian Society, which would care for any "Jewish children of the submerged" committed through the courts, whether orphaned or not. With the help of an all-woman board of managers and an all-male advisory committee headed by Judge Joachimsen, the new society rented a former city councilman's home in a semi-rural, suburban section of the city at 57th Street and First Avenue, and prepared to admit children from two to 13. *All* the initial children — whether orphaned or not — came through the courts, because the HSGS could only bill the city for these. Not until 1888 was it chartered as an orphanage.

It was with pride that its president proclaimed on the day of the opening: "We have to take care and nurse the neglected and abandoned Jewish children because we are *Jewesses*."

The *New York Herald* printed her speech in full. But the *Jewish Messenger* greeted the occasion with marked distrust. Women were not considered capable of managing money, much less the public funds on which the institution expected largely to depend.

The fact of a woman president did not deter applicants. In its first year, the new institution received 276 requests for admission and accepted 164 children. Its running costs that year exceeded the public per capita subsidy by 23%. For many years its most important sources for meeting such deficits were donations (never considerable) and an annual benefit ball. The charity box in the entrance hall was a dud. It never yielded more than $100 a year.

The program designed by the women managers was very simple. Within the orphanage walls, the children ate and slept, the youngest had their "Kinder-Garden", and the older children their religious education. But the children were to be as little isolated from the outside world as possible. Both the HSGS and the HOA fervently believed in "americanising" their little wards at all costs, short of the sacrifice of Judaism.

Children who were old enough attended the local public schools. And, for maximum exposure and to win support for the orphanage's work, the five local synagogues were visited in rotation on the Sabbath. Since there was little play room inside the orphanage, recreation also was sought in the neighborhood outside. Thanks to the generosity of owners of nearby beaches, the pure, clean East River was available for swimming. A harbor towing company regularly made available a boat for excursions, and so, occasionally, did the City's Commissioner of Charities and Corrections. Bloomingdale Brothers nearby provided Chanukah entertainments, and there were outings to the parks and to Long Island beaches.

The outside world was welcome to visit — any day from 11 to 4. (Only the child's own family was limited to a single weekend day each month!) When there was room in the Kinder-Garden class, neighborhood tots could attend. And there were always the needy dropping in for a free meal. Many of these were young Jewish girls who worked for very low pay in local stores and whose homes were too far away to return to for lunch. In the depression year of 1885, 5,892 free meals were served by the HSGS.

At first, the lady managers were closely involved in the running of the institution. Every day one came, on a rotating schedule, to supervise the work of the paid superintendent, the matron, and the "servants," while the ladies of the Josephine Sewing Society stitched away, providing clothing and linens.

The board met weekly. No child was discharged by the managers without careful preliminary investigation. A board member always visited the place of business or the home before a boy was placed out as an apprentice or a girl to learn housekeeping. Follow-up ended with the initial investigation of a child's progress and adjustment, but graduates were warmly invited to drop by for a bite on a Sabbath evening — or at any time for help and advice.

This intimate arrangement was short-lived. The HSGS home had been open only a few months when the first wave of Jewish refugees from Czarist Russia struck the city. Wave after wave followed as more Jews fled the pogroms and discriminatory laws that were turning life in Eastern Europe into a hell for the Children of Israel. In 1870, New York's 80,000 Jews were 9% of the city's population. By 1907, thirty-seven years later, more than that number would be coming off the boats *every year,* and the Jewish population would reach one million or 25% of the total.

On they came, the penniless newcomers, seeking that new life promised in America. But the life most of them found was the seamy side of the American dream. Packed into narrow East Side tenements, toiling from dawn to dusk in the sweatshops, many an immigrant family soon was torn by stress and illness. Tuberculosis and mental breakdowns took a particularly heavy toll among the Jews. Husbands or wives — often in precarious health —

were left to raise children alone; deserted and orphaned children to forage in the streets.

The German-Jewish population of New York — by now socially the dominant Jewish group — was stunned at the sudden presence of so many impoverished, hard-pressed "relatives." What had the two groups in common besides their religion? Even there, vast differences yawned between the reform or reform-influenced rituals of the established New York Jews and the strict orthodoxy of the more recent arrivals. As if to drive the wedge deeper, the German Jews were beginning to encounter anti-semitism in the once-tolerant city.

As early as 1877, banker and former HOA president Joseph Seligman and his party had suffered the shock of their lives when they were turned away from the formerly hospitable Grand Union Hotel in Saratoga because the hotel had decided no longer to admit Jews. By 1893, the last wraps were off. The following unabashed description of the Lower East Side in the *New York Times* of July 30 reflects the attitude of many:

> "This neighborhood, peopled almost entirely by the people who claim to have been driven from Poland and Russia, is the eyesore of New York and perhaps the filthiest place on the western continent. It is impossible for a Christian to live there because he will be driven out, either by blows or the dirt and stench. . . . They cannot be lifted up to a higher plane because they do not want to be."

Like well-established people anywhere, the German Jews tended to blame these distressing new attitudes on those who suffered from them the most — in this case the poverty-stricken new arrivals. But there was no ignoring the fact that rich and poor were all members of the same Jewish nation. The need of the newcomers for the "charity that also means justice" had to be met.

By 1880, the board of the Hebrew Orphan Asylum was poring over plans for a larger structure and had purchased a two-block site between 136th and 138th Streets on Amsterdam Avenue.

But fund-raising for the new building was held up in order not to compete with the desperate need for immigrant relief. The HOA board resolved "The building could be postponed, but the feeding of the hungry and aiding of the helpless could not brook delay."

Nevertheless, by October 1884, a vast structure with a marbled front hall had been erected at the new site and the children moved in. Repeatedly enlarged to accommodate need, the new HOA would one day care for 1755 children.

Meanwhile the doors of the HSGS on 57th Street were barely opened when it was found necessary to add a three-story brick wing. Next, it leased an annex a few doors away, where it installed its girls and two to six year olds. By 1884, it had four separate buildings in the neighborhood and had moved the girls and infants to a handsome mansion at East 87th Street and York Avenue, once owned by John Jacob Astor. "The separation of the sexes by location in independent and disconnected buildings is indispensable," firmly stated Mrs. Joachimsen in her annual report.

But it proved impossible to supervise so many separate buildings. In 1887 the number was reduced to two by moving the boys and infants to the former "Union Home and School for Children of Our Soldiers and Sailors" located at Grand Drive (now Broadway), Western Boulevard (Riverside Drive), and 150th to 151st Streets. (This institution, too, had had an all-woman board, including such luminous names as Mrs. "General" Grant and Mrs. "Admiral" Farragut.) Although the property had little outdoor space of its own, broad neighboring fields sloped down to the Hudson. It seemed at the time there would always be plenty of room for play. And the interior had been recently renovated, even to modern plumbing with hot and cold water and "sinks and closets of the most approved kind."

In 1892, an annex was completed for the girls next to the boys' building (further reducing the play area), and they, too, were moved uptown. By 1893, the two HSGS units between them housed 800 children.

Across the river, the Brooklyn orphanage was suffering similar growing pains. The former rented building had long since been purchased, along with 35 adjacent lots, and several times enlarged. But for a while, after the completion of the huge new HOA asylum, there *had* been the hope that Manhattan would take Brooklyn back. December 15, 1889, that hope was dispelled. Brooklyn president Leo Bamberger and another board member met with the HOA board to discuss turning over the Brooklyn assets and Brooklyn children to the HOA. But the HOA president, Jesse Seligman, and his board felt they would very soon need the room themselves. "We are therefore brought face to face with the stern reality of the situation," wrote the Brooklyn president in his 1890 report. "The care of the Jewish orphans of the County of Kings will rest for many years with us."

In 1892, a cornerstone was laid for the huge new Brooklyn asylum at Ralph and Howard Avenues, Dean and Pacific Streets that would for many years be known as "The House on the Hill." The former property was sold, and the children moved. At its peak the new orphanage would care for 1,200 children.

One age gap remained unfilled. The babies. Traditionally boarded out with wet-nurses, these usually came to the HSGS when they turned two. But in the struggle against contagious diseases that characterized this period, wet-nurses were falling into disfavor. An institution again seemed to be the answer. In 1895, the Hebrew Infants Asylum opened with five babies in a spacious and airy house at East 149th Street and Mott Avenue in the Bronx. It was prepared to care for 34 children, from birth to five years of age — but only those fortunate enough to have been "born in wedlock" were entitled to care during the asylum's early years.

By the standards of their day, just how successful were all these Jewish orphanages in caring for their destitute or orphaned charges?

Children *everywhere* were expected first of all to be obedient and respect their elders, to be seen and not heard. Even adults in the nineteenth century were not to expect too much joy out of life. The rules and regulations of the Mount Sinai Training Center for Nurses placed in the cornerstone box of the HOA's Amsterdam Avenue Building, in 1883, cautions the nursing student: "Remember that this is the world of work; the next is the world of recompense."

Such stern philosophies of course were made sterner in the orphanages by the harsh necessity of caring for hundreds of children under one roof, with one adult "keeper" to every 100 "inmates." Regimentation and suppression of individual personality were the order of the day. Yet, considering this, the success of the Jewish orphanages in many ways seems to have been remarkable. Certainly, official praise for their efforts was never lacking.

A *New York Times* reporter touring the city's orphanages in 1869 was critical of most of those he saw. They seemed to him for the most part dank and dark — a sort of grim boarding school, "with no home to look back or forward to; no holidays or vacations . . . but year after year of the strange unnatural school life." However, he found the HOA (then located on 77th Street) "one of the most elegant buildings of its kind in the city and, unlike some of the others, it has halls and apartments comfortably heated." It seemed "rather a *home* for the children than a boarding school, and" he noted approvingly, "they are all sent to the public schools."

In 1876, a year after the passage of the Children's Law, the noted philanthropist and commissioner of the New York State Board of Charities, William P. Letchworth, visited 130 child-caring institutions to see if they were, in fact, any better than the almshouses. Although finding many defects, he concluded the children's institutions definitely were to be preferred. And he voiced particular approval of the "thoroughness of the work being done and the zeal actuating the workers" of the HOA.

The president of the New York Society for the Prevention of Cruelty to Children could not praise the Jewish effort enough. He repeatedly expressed "unqualified admiration." "With all my experience in the management of institutions for the benefit of children," wrote Elbridge T. Gerry to the HOA president, "I have yet to find any which compare with those in charge of your people."

"I only wish," he wrote the HSGS president, Priscilla Joachimsen in 1887, "that the example which your institution has set would be followed by others, because your system demonstrates how easily and how well children may be cared for where proper officers are selected, proper buildings procured, and a proper supervision given to the entire work by persons of intelligence and education."

The first thing any visitor remarked was the wax-clean interior of the Jewish institutions and the spotless attire of the children. The huge dormitories, where 100 beds were lined up with scarcely any space between, were always in perfect order. The inspectors of the city's Department of Charities and Corrections repeatedly gave the Jewish orphanages top rating for their "sanitary" housekeeping.

In that day, before inoculations and vaccines (save against smallpox), and before miracle drugs, where hundreds of children were massed together, cleanliness and order were a life and death necessity. But many orphanages failed conspicuously to maintain high standards. Never the Jewish asylums. The ever-present fear of contagious sickness runs like a taut threat through the annual reports. Superintendents fervently thank God that "the sanitary condition of our children is excellent," or boast "no child lost during the past year by death."

The health records *were* astounding. In 1922, HOA president Joseph Newburger, looking back to the founding of the first orphan's home, could say that of 13,506 children admitted during the 62 years only 62 had died while in the institution's care. An average of one death a year.

Such laurels were hard won. From the opening of its first orphan's home in 1860, the medical board of the HOA was headed by Dr. Abraham Jacobi, a man recognized today as the founder of American pediatrics. His compaign to improve the health of children included the struggle for compulsory vaccination against smallpox, investigations into diphtheria (which at the time took the lives of 60 to 80% of those under two whom it attacked); and a long battle against the common practice of bleeding children.

The German-born doctor with the stunted body and huge head also fought for pure milk ("Heat it until you see the bubbles."), and argued fervently for the breast-feeding of infants which, at the time, was being supplanted by the newly fashionable bottle. A founder of Mount Sinai Hospital and for many years president of its medical board, he was also the first president of the American Pediatrics Society and the first professor of pediatrics in the United States. He served the orphans of the HOA without pay for 60 years.

The rules and regulations he drew up for the house physician of the HOA in 1868 required a "daily or oftener if necessary" visit to the asylum; a "thorough inspection of the physical condition of all the children" at least once a month; and meticulous record keeping. The "Attending Physician" — for many years Dr. Jacobi himself — was to visit at least once a week, supervise the house physician and check his records.

State law did not require an orphanage to employ a regular doctor to examine newly admitted children and supervise health care until 1886. But both the HOA and the HSGS from their opening day required all children to be examined and vaccinated by an attending physician on admittance and their health regularly checked. The HSGS had a medical board of five, its first year. However, it was only after 1886, in conformity with a law passed that year, that three-week quarantines appear to have been imposed on new arrivals.

The quarantines were long overdue. Even with this extra precaution, the contagious children's diseases, gonorrheal vaginitis, and dirt-borne eye and skin infections sometimes got a head start in the dormitories. Once started, they could rage for months. The test could hardly be an institution's success in excluding such diseases but the energy with which it engaged the enemy once the infection was recognized. Every resource of the Jewish institutions was hurled into battle.

In 1886, eye diseases attacked 118 children at the HSGS. The Board reported overcoming the infliction "without injury to any of our children" but only through "the great care of our Doctors, special employment of competent oculists, and of a large number of professionally trained nurses." In 1895, when one-half of the 800 HSGS children developed the dreaded ringworm of the scalp, there was no hiding the sick children in the basement as one notorious orphanage had done. The desperate president instead called the Board of Health to investigate. The outcome was the forced resignation of the attending physician who had been careless in his admissions practices.

Three years later, dysentery felled 159 of the 865 children at the HOA. Again, no time was wasted. The institution was closed, the children transferred, and the water and sewage systems overhauled in an effort to determine the cause — a tainted water supply due to a fault in the city water main. Seven children had died.

That summer the alarmed HSGS boiled every drop of drinking water and confined all its children to the institution. No picnics or outings for them.

Epidemics were anxiously described in the annual reports, and professional papers on such problems as vaginitis were sometimes bound into the brown leather volumes of the HSGS reports. But space was also found for small triumphs.

In 1894, the HSGS jubilantly reported the total recovery of a girl of 10 and a boy of 9, both of whom had been almost blind due to years of severe conjunctivitis. In 1886, a five-year-old was brought in "in a most infirm and crippled condition." The child had been denied admission to other institutions as incurable. But the lady managers of the HSGS reported that "by great attention and minute care" the little girl regained perfect good health and the full use of her limbs and "is a very bright child!" The same report described a full orphan "about 7" who had been pro-nounced an incurable mute. After failing to place the boy in a special institution, the lady managers gave him "all the attention in our power with the happy result that speech is coming slowly but surely."

After 1870, the HOA was particularly fortunate in having the backup services of Dr. Jacobi's hospital, Mount Sinai. That year, when a Hebrew Charity Fair raised more than $100,000 for the benefit of the two Jewish institutions, the HOA — its needs being less — gracefully offered to cede two-thirds of the proceeds to the hospital. In return, Mount Sinai agreed to set aside a ward for the free care of any HOA children requiring hospital services. The agreement, although not implemented by a separate ward, re-mained in force for many decades, until public subsidies for hos-pital care rendered it unnecessary.

Tender loving care obviously was not absent. Only the dental practices of the day seem to have lacked it completely.

Undoubtedly the 262 extractions performed by Dr. David Kreisler at the HSGS in 1899 could partially be blamed on years of prior neglect and malnutrition. But his science was still in the dark ages. "A man would come with a pair of pliers and yank out any decayed teeth from a long line of frightened children," ex-plains one HOA report, while "old Ma Ferman held a basin under the chin of each child." And oh, how "the howling and shrieking of the first in line terrorized those that followed."

Education was another notable concern of the Jewish children's institutions. The trustees of the HOA in 1866 complained to the editor of the *Jewish Messenger* of the many children placed in the asylum for only a few years and then removed by their parents:

"An erroneous impression apparently prevails among the mass of the community as to the objects of the asylum which are misconstrued to represent the purposes of an educational institute in which the children are supposed to acquire for a few years intellectual and physical culture."

Mrs. Joachimsen's first annual report was explicit about the HSGS' intentions: "In accordance with the law of this state, the institution will receive, care for and EDUCATE such Jewish children as may be committed to its care. . . ." The lady managers saw to it that their charges trudged daily to the neighborhood public schools. They also appealed regularly to the community for scholarship funds for more advanced education for their more promising wards. But, alas, in the nineteenth century such funds were not easily obtained by a board of women.

The HOA, always more fortunate where money was concerned, received its first scholarship endowment in 1891 when Jacob H. Schiff initiated what was to become probably the most heavily endowed educational fund of any American orphanage. His $16,500 was to be used to help HOA wards "take up study of some profession which is not commercial in its character, preference to be given to a boy who chooses an artistic or scientific career."

With their shaved heads and the severely plain clothing always purchased in job lots, the children of all three orphanages were easily recognized on the streets or at school. Lower East Side teachers frequently expressed astonishment at the eagerness to learn of most Jewish children. But the institutional children had particular cause for eagerness. One HSGS alumnus, Michael Sharlitt, recalled later of those years with no summer camps and few outings: "School meant everything to me. I disliked as others must have the long vacation which meant the monotony of the daily institutional regime." Another explained: "Our lack of confidence was mastered only by the will to succeed."

But Alexander Smith, the brother of publisher Peter Smith, recalls a more positive reason for scholarly ambition at the HSGS: "We were surrounded by more than our share of gifted and dedicated teachers." The Washington Heights community at that time was an affluent, semi-rural one with many country squires. Its schools were among the city's best.

The supporters of the orphanages preferred to have the children sent to the public schools, considering this an essential way to Americanize them. Originally, the HOA had conformed to this practice. But in 1884, when it moved its 368 children to the new building at 136th Street and Amsterdam, it discovered the schools of the neighborhood could not accommodate the sudden influx.

So the HOA opened a school within its walls. At first it provided classes only for its youngest children. But as the population grew, both inside and outside the walls, further classes were added until all children through grade six attended school on the orphanage premises. In 1904, a liberalizing administration turned the school within the walls over to the Board of Education and it became P.S. 192. Thereafter, neighborhood children attended the primary grades in the orphanage building along with the wards of the HOA, while both groups of older children continued to go to school outside, as they had always done.

A school within the walls had certain advantages. The children did not have to miss class every time the orphanage was quarantined. In 1890, even before its move to the "House on the Hill," the Brooklyn institution, too, considered adding an intra-mural school for that reason. "I am informed," said the worried president in his report, "that a rule has been recently enacted that all pupils attending public school from any charitable institution will be compelled to refrain from such attendance if, in such institution, one or more cases of contagious disease prevail. If this rule be enforced, it will readily be seen how much valuable time would necessarily be lost to all the orphans. . . ." At the time the BHOA only had 96 "inmates." Six years later, in its new building, there were 293. But the school within the walls never materialized.

The unflagging concern of all the Jewish orphanages for the education of their young naturally brought results. In 1887, HOA Superintendent Hermann Baar proudly announced that of 170 older children sent to the public school, 166 had been rated excellent or good and only four "indifferent." The Superintendent made special mention of Sarah Frank —"one of the best and most well-behaved girls that ever was brought up in an institution."

Well, yes, there were exceptions. And they, too, were noted, but with less pleasure. The HOA School Detention Book for 1879 to 1884 posts their names. Moses Anschel earned steady disapproval. "Very disorderly conduct." "Poor, poor, poor." "Gave a great deal of trouble." Nothing in the entire book stands out quite so ominously as the *"Very Bad"* noted in large black letters next to the boy's name on March 11, 1879.

Technical training was another early concern of the trustees of the Jewish institutions. It was essential that their wards be taught to earn a living. And the old indenture system of placing a boy or girl out to learn a trade was falling into disrepute. It permitted too many abuses.

Remember Henry Bauer? There was no technical training at the HOA in Henry's day. Discharged in 1864, he was apprenticed to a silver-tongued fellow who took him upstate to Plattsburg. There he was handed a heavy glass case to hang around his neck and sent into the barracks to sell cigars to Union soldiers. Not much of a trade.

When some goods disappeared, several months later, the master falsely blamed Henry. He slapped him in the face and sent a letter to the institution describing the boy as "the most naughty" he ever had and asking to trade him in for a better model.

The trustees' reply was routine and stern. Satisfied or not, the boy's "master and guardian" was responsible for the boy's welfare.

Poor Henry! He had already been put on a train to New York, but he knew the orphanage rule better than his master. So off he had jumped and gone off with some soldiers, bound for the battlefields of the South. Many years and many adventures later, he ended up the nightwatchman at the great orphange on Amsterdam Avenue, where, in 1910, he was interviewed by a reporter from *The American Hebrew.*

Not all apprenticeships turned out so poorly, of course, although some turned out even worse. And there were always special cases where the orphanage would retain an over-age ward to help further his or her education. This was the case with Betsy Brock who, at the special request of her principal, was kept in the HOA past the usual dismissal age of 14 so she could finish high school and become a public school teacher.

The HOA began providing vocational education as early as 1869 when it installed a "Master of the Shoe Factory" to "well and truly instruct such boys as the Board of Governors shall see fit to have instructed in the art, trade or mastery of boot and shoe making."

By 1872, a print shop had been added and a building erected to serve as an industrial school. The *Minutes* of 1873 further disclose an offer to teach the girls umbrella and parasol making. This was being favorably entertained.

The HOA's industrial school was discontinued when the HOA moved to the huge new building on Amsterdam Avenue. The Hebrew Technical Institute for Boys had been founded in 1883, under the leadership of HOA trustee James H. Hoffman. Now the institute obligingly moved to a location closer to the HOA, so the orphanage's eligible boys could continue their studies there after graduating from the elementary school. The HOA partially financed the technical institute's move by promising a substantial sum toward the rent. Many HSGS boys also attended this school.

Of course there were disadvantages to sending boys past 14 to be trained outside the walls of the institutions. In 1903, the HSGS superintendent bemoaned the tendency of destitute families to reclaim such children — in order to send them "anywhere where they can earn something."

In later years girls were sometimes sent to the Hebrew Technical School for Girls to learn dressmaking, cooking or office skills. Originally opened in 1884 as the Louis Downtown Sabbath School for Girls, this was an outgrowth of a sewing circle for girls from the Lower East Side started by Minnie D. Louis in 1880. But the school was far from the orphanages — on East Fifteenth Street. In earlier years, less advanced needlework and cooking courses were taught at the orphanages themselves. In this respect, Mrs. Joachimsen boasted in 1887, the HSGS was "practically an industrial school." But actually it never had the space to provide much technical training.

Musical training was a strong feature of the educational programs, with its earliest and most popular form the band. This suited both the children's need for recreation and the administration's love of military order. The marching bands of the Jewish orphanages were famous and never lacked engagements, although sometimes earning the stiff disapproval of the more orthodox for their ecumenical willingness to play at Catholic and Protestant benefits.

The bands won many awards. The most spectacular of these was the first prize blue banner brought home from the Washington Centennial Parade, in 1889, by the HOA band. Civil War hero General William Tecumseh Sherman — a longtime friend of HOA president Jesse Seligman — arrived at the orphanage in person along with two other generals to make the official presentation. The day, according to the *New York Times,* was topped by a turkey banquet followed by enough ice cream and cake to "sink a ship."

If true, it was better thanks than ever was earned by the equally renowned HSGS band. Although they played 40 concerts a year and turned down more, the boys had a saying that all they ever got in return was "a toothpick and a glass of water." In their white-trimmed grey uniforms and grey soldier hats, the 30 boys were the star performers at the dedication of Grant's Tomb in 1890. But eventually the administration had to curtail their activities to prevent indiscriminate exploitation.

Of play, there was little in the nineteenth century. Hebrew classes took up so much of the free period after school that even the elderly and pious Dr. Baar was known to worry about how little time was left for anything else.

With no equipment, children had to be ingenious. The same one-piece swimming suit could serve a boy in the morning, a girl in the afternoon. Old cast-off basins would do in winter for belly-whopping down the slopes behind the HSGS. And the crowded, brick-paved playground saw many games of "oyster sale," "prisoners base," and "one-two-three old cat." Running trunks were pillow cases with the corners cut off. And balls could be improvised from unravelled cotton covered with strips of sheet and sewn with shoelaces. Sometimes, 100 boys kept 20 balls flying at a time. A miracle none were ever hurt.

And the children — how did they feel living in these great nineteenth century orphan barracks? Only the alumni can reply.

Former New York State Parole Commissioner Aaron Jacoby, currently a trustee of the JCCA, entered the HOA with his brother in 1903 at six years of age and later headed the Brooklyn institution (BHOA). He recalls he had a "very happy childhood." But he remembers the merciless bullying of the boy monitors appointed to keep order. With only one paid adult "governor"— as the supervisors by then were called — to every 100 children, order depended on older wards who exerted almost unlimited tyranny. They also earned bitter envy for having the right to grow their cropped hair a *bit* longer in front.

The HSGS president in 1896 stated that corporal punishment had at all times been forbidden in the institution and "we have strictly adhered to our rules forbidding it." And at no time did the institution get any income from the labor of "inmates." But HSGS alumna Amelia Davis recalls a supervisor named Piggy of about that period who went about with a metal ruler suspended from her belt and used it unmercifully. The same woman forced the little girls to make scarves and doilies which she then sold on the outside. Who would have dared complain?

The underpaid supervisors for the girls were for the most part unhappy young Catholic women —"fresh off the pickle boats" from Poland. Mrs. Davis recalls their morning ritual for awakening their little charges — a mass rush and a yank at the sheets that rolled a sleeping child onto the floor.

These were the hidden miseries. But other customs at least as cruel were openly tolerated, in line with the child care philosophy of that day. Children who wet their beds — and they were many — were forced to stand in one corner of the dining room at breakfast with the wet sheets draped over their shoulders. (Although at least one supervisor preferred to punish enuretic boys by forcing them to wear a girl's dress.)

In 1882, the city paid $110 per year for each child committed to an orphanage. About thirty cents a day. The sheer necessity of caring for so many children on so little money meant that salaries were rock-bottom and personnel, as Michael Sharlitt recalled of the HSGS, "for the most part escapees from the rigid competition of life. I fail to recall a single person who had the barest preparation for the work, except for the doctor and the nurse."

Food costs were "close to a daring minimum. Many who left the institution at the legal working age of 14 were actually stunted," he says.

Yet emotionally — and even physically — threadbare though so much of it seemed, many alumni recall a more positive side to orphanage life. "We were disadvantaged," says one Brooklyn alumnus, "*before* we arrived at 373 Ralph Avenue." Clean laundry, plenty of heat from the boiler room, clarinet lessons, regular if unsatisfying meals, medical care, an occasional nickel fare salvaged by walking instead of riding — these were not to be scorned by children coming from the streets of the congested tenements of the New York ghetto. "At least the home gave us a fresh start," said future publisher Peter Smith.

And there were always a few legendary board members to improve the quality of orphan life. Such a one was Seligman Solomon who daily visited the HOA from 1868 to his death in 1885. It was never the outstanding child he noticed, but the little one too shy to ask for attention. When the children went out into the world, he followed them. He helped them get positions, visited their employers to see that they were adequately paid and made sure they were properly clothed. In the Orphans' Plot at Salem Fields Cemetery where he had asked to be buried, the former HOA wards erected a monument to his name. And when they formed their first alumni society in 1887 — to help each other as he had helped them — they named it the Seligman Solomon Society.

But with or without help, the purposeful vitality of the Lower East Side was not easily crushed. The small market of negotiable orphan possessions could be cornered by a sharp-witted youngster like Peter Smith — with money improvised from spent cartridge shells picked up at a shooting gallery. Hairs stolen from the tails of delivery horses made saleable rings and bracelets. Rings also could be manufactured from ground-down cherry pits dipped in colored inks. These wares could be sold discreetly to outsiders, building the confidence of a young entrepreneur.

The orphanage administrations, too, had high hopes for their charges. A four-year-old waif rescued from a Christian institution, where he had routinely been named "John Doe No. 19," was swiftly handed the name "Judah Touro," after the great American-Jewish philanthropist. Who knew, perhaps he would do as well. In the seventies, four of Horatio Alger's early books were serialized in the HOA magazine, *Young Israel.* The sky was the limit for the Jewish orphan.

But institutional life spelled death to many a family tie. As the institutions grew, parents' visiting days were further reduced. What had been one day every month, became one in every two months at the HSGS, one in every three at the HOA.

There were real problems. The fear of contagious diseases, the large number of children. But the truth was that the improverished, Yiddish-speaking immigrant parent was considered rather a hindrance than a help — a potential barrier to the steady upward mobility every orphanage so feverently wished for its charges. Visitors from more affluent neighborhoods, on the other hand, were always welcome. They were probably healthy and perhaps they would contribute to the work. But the parent was of quite a different background than the predominantly German or English trustee or institutional executive. There was little empathy for the poor.

Children who knew only English became strangers to their families. Even brothers and sisters, living for years in separate wings of the same institution, grew far apart. One alumnus recalls the monthly brother-sister meetings of a later date, that were designed to overcome this alienation, as "merely embarrassing." After years apart, he and his sister no longer had anything to say to one another.

But shared pain had its positive side. "The love everlasting that one Home kid has for another," wrote one BHOA alumnus, "is impossible for outside kids to understand."

Every orphanage ward knew what it was to cry him or herself to sleep at night in a dormitory that held 100 to 200 identical beds — but quietly so the monitor wouldn't notice and punish. Many could recall the sight of weeping grandmothers, pleading not to have all that beautiful hair shaved off. Or the shame of oversize trousers or dresses taken in with a safety pin. The trousers were so strong it took six boys to wear out one suit. And those shoes outgrown by other orphans! They never quite fitted.

Every child knew the joy of the rare family visiting day — when there was a family. Or the tears when no one came. More than one could recall a cigar-maker father who had contracted tuberculosis in the foul sweat shop and would never kiss his child on visiting day because he "had a cold." And the mothers trying to hide the candy and fruit they were not supposed to bring.

*Every* child had received the help and understanding of those who understood most perfectly — other children in the same situation. "Being part of a mass gave me a feeling of belonging," wrote one BHOA alumnus. "For every older fellow ready to beat me up, there was one who patted me on the back and gave me a lift when I needed it."

And there were the shared "happenings". The day in January, 1881, when the HSGS was set on fire by an "insane incendiary who perished miserably in the flames she had kindled." (The superintendent and matron fortunately put out the flames before any child was injured.) And the panic created at the BHOA asylum during the Spanish-American War, when the flagpole was shattered by lightning — with the children all crying that "Spaniards was bombing the orphan asylum."

Were the institutionalized Jewish children so much worse off than those in struggling families on the outside? As a child, Harry Roskolenko knew the HOA only as a picture in a souvenir album of the Educational Alliance, and dreaded the thought he might have to go there. Yet, he wrote later, ". . . on the East Side we were all orphans in some strange way."

Nevertheless, by the turn of the century there was a growing recognition that the barracks-system of caring for children had turned into a monster. To make ends meet, every institution had to remain filled to capacity, because every additional child committed by the city cut down the overhead. Children were staying longer and longer because no one had time or inclination to find out if their family situation had changed and if they could be released to their relatives.

In 1875, only eight percent of all children committed to an institution stayed more than five years. By 1894, the figure staying five or more years was twenty-three percent. "Inaction is more natural than action," wrote William P. Letchworth in 1893, "and when children are once received into these institutions, it is easier to allow them to remain there indefinitely. . . . So time slips away; and the child grows up in the institution when it would have been better fitted to struggle with the world had it been early restored to family life."

By the time the children of the orphanages returned to their communities they were rootless strangers.

Yet, in 1893, with 700 children under a roof built to shelter 500, the only remedy discussed by the HOA Board was the addition of two more wings. The venerable Dr. Baar suspected this was "a step in the wrong direction."

"We cannot," he said, "compare the Catholic Protectory, which contains 2,000 children, with ours. The children of that institution, more or less depraved, are placed under rigorous measures and restraints, whilst our children have to be ruled with persuasion and gentle means."

"Gentlemen," the superintendent pleaded to the trustees, "excuse the liberty I have taken in addressing you in this manner. With 700 children in the house, we have already in the better sense of the word a so-called 'machine-education'; if you take several hundred more . . . you will reduce the Asylum, pardon my expression, to a mere boarding establishment."

He admitted his objection would have been less strenuous if the contemplated building were to be a separate house for the girls. Although girls and boys inhabited different sides of the building, and although they ate in different sections of the dining hall, the HOA superintendent sighed at the impossibility of preventing contact between the grown-up girls and boys. "We have often found correspondence between the sexes," he complained. In an effort to cut expenses, the HOA had entrusted the girls with all the housework, even to making the boys' beds. This had the saving grace of providing daring opportunities to slip love notes between sheets.

Despite Dr. Baar's sensible remonstrances, the two new wings planned for 500 more children were completed by the HOA in 1896. Four years later, the HSGS — bursting at *its* mortar seams with 925 children — launched a campaign to raise $250,000 for an annex which it pessimistically expected would satisfy its needs only for another ten years.

And after ten years — what? By the end of the century, the majority of child care experts and professionals no longer believed that huge institutions were the best way to care for orphaned or destitute children.

Fortunately for the Jewish orphans of New York, winds of change were blowing in the fields of child care.

# Chapter 3

# The Changing of the Guard

*"We have arrived at that stage of our existence when something more should be done than merely clothe, feed, and plainly educate."*
SAMUEL D. LEVY, 24th ANNUAL REPORT OF THE HEBREW SHELTERING GUARDIAN SOCIETY, OCTOBER 1, 1903.

THE FIRST SIGNS OF CHANGE noticed by the wards of the Jewish orphanages must have been the new faces that suddenly appeared on their scene around the turn of the century. One by one the old guard were dying or retiring, and younger men were taking their place. The newcomers naturally were more sensitive than the old to the new ideas concerning child-rearing and social welfare gaining ground during their own lifetimes. It was, in general, a propitious time for ideas. It was a time of reform in America.

Many concerned men and women long had known that a child was not just a miniature adult, but a developing individual with special needs and special problems. Now welfare services and laws, too, were beginning to reflect this knowledge.

As early as 1886, Josephine Shaw Lowell of the State Board of Charities had drafted a bill to set up a municipal bureau devoted exclusively to children. Her bill had not passed. But other progress had been realized. Day nurseries and visiting nurse services had appeared to service children and their families, the last child had left the state's almshouses, and in faraway Cook County, Illinois, the first children's court had been established in 1899.

Education, too, was changing. Psychologists had rejected the learning by rote which, for centuries, had been considered the only way to teach a child. A child should learn by doing, not from words, they said. One educator, John Dewey, even insisted on treating boys and girls alike. In his school, both sexes took courses in cooking, sewing, and carpentry.

The foster home movement had had its crude beginnings in 1853 in Charles Loring Brace's efforts to place homeless children with families in the West. His concept had been heavily debated during the last half of the nineteenth century. But although most child welfare leaders by 1900 supported family care of some sort as opposed to institutional care, it would be a while before the institutions felt the competition of the new movement. Nevertheless the idea was there to draw on.

Finally, the thought that professional skills were necessary in order to truly help people in trouble had gained steadily in acceptance, since the nineties when the Charity Organization Societies first had pioneered the hiring of professionals to train and supervise its volunteers. In 1898, the New York society had even opened a "training school for philanthropic work" (now the Columbia University School of Social Work). The State Board of Charities hailed the step in these words:

"Such efforts as these are cordially welcomed by the Board, for in the civilization of today, which is rapidly growing more complex, and presenting problems difficult of analysis, it is important that those who seek to benefit the poor should act with wisdom born of knowledge, and that careless and haphazard methods should not have countenance or support." To raise the standards of the institutions under its own jurisdiction, the board itself in the late nineties had introduced such measures as civil service, the merit system and salary-classification.

It was against this background of social welfare ferment and change that the new guard entered the Jewish orphanages.

In 1899, after 23 years, the venerable Dr. Herman Baar vacated the superintendent's suite at the HOA. A few years later, a former rabbi named Solomon Loewenstein moved his family in. Where Dr. Baar had found 300 children, in 1876, at 77th Street, Dr. Loewenstein now found 1,000 in the two-block orphan city at 136th Street and Amsterdam Avenue.

"Dear, beloved Dr. Baar," the silver-haired pedagogue who had ruled the HOA with Germanic discipline and benevolence, was replaced by a youthful superintendent with a more knowledgeable approach to the problems of child welfare, one who planned a career in the new social service profession.

His assistant represented yet another type of administrator, equally new to the world of the barracks. A former ward of the

HOA, Lionel Simmonds knew intimately what it was like to grow up in a large congregate institution.

Within a few years, another former HOA ward would head the Brooklyn Hebrew Orphan Asylum. When first promoted to super-intendent, Aaron L. Jacoby was a precocious 24.

But it was the children at the third of the great Jewish asylums whose lives were most transformed in the first fifteen years of the twentieth century. Fortunately for them, the HSGS was the most ripe of the three for change.

Alone of the three, it desperately needed a new building. The other two had designed and built the plants in which their children now lived. But the rundown, overcrowded HSGS, with its peeling paint, its cramped playground, and lack of indoor facilities, was frankly inadequate. It was a time to rethink old programs and plan all-encompassing improvements. And the deaths of Priscilla and Philip Joachimsen, in the early nineties, had left a void soon to be filled by new and vigorous initiative.

Mrs. Joachimsen and her hard-working board of women managers had exhausted themselves in years of attempting to cope with the waves of immigrant children for whom they had been so little prepared. After their president's death, and a brief interim admin-istration under Morris Goodhart, the worried board called in an energetic 35-year old lawyer who once had served as the HSGS' first secretary.

Samuel D. Levy had been only 17 in 1879 and a student at City College. In the intervening years he had earned a law degree and for 14 years had served on the board of the United Hebrew Charities. There he had provided free legal aid to the poor and to children charged with their first crimes. Those years of service had taught Levy much about the needs and problems of the chil-dren committed to the orphanage on Grand Boulevard.

The managers begged Samuel Levy to take over the presidency of the HSGS. He accepted, on condition he have a free hand to make any changes he considered necessary, and announced that the goal of his administration would be the "individualizing" of each child.

But individualizing required money. And the institution Levy had been called in to rescue was, as he phrased it, the "Cinderella" of the Jewish orphanages. Its managers had been timid fund-raisers. Unlike the HOA, with its prestigious all-male board, they had never solicited dues-paying "patrons, subscribers, and members," but had tried to make up their yearly deficit through private contributions and annual fund-raising benefits.

Levy wryly acknowledged that the $110 a year per committed child paid by the city might be enough "if our object was merely keeping the child alive and then setting it adrift at 15 or 16 years. But our duties are greater and more solemn. We ought not to discharge a child without that mental, moral, physical and spiritual reserve and stamina so vital to its future well-being . . . to become a useful member — nay, an ornament! — to society."

With what envy must Levy have eyed the HOA, whose president, Emanuel Lehman, had recently celebrated his seventieth birthday by endowing a $100,000 fund for the higher education of that asylum's charges.

Fortunately for the HSGS wards, the turn of the century was a propitious time to interest men of wealth in philanthropic enterprise. By 1890 there were more than 4,047 millionaires in the United States, and Andrew Carnegie had made fashionable the idea that these should employ their money to benefit society while they lived.

Carnegie's thinking perfectly suited the Jewish tradition. But there were other turn-of-the century influences such as the muckracking journalists who exposed to the reading public the sufferings of the poor. One, Jacob Riis, had taken a camera into the slums and recorded unforgettably how that "other half" lived.

Soon, at Levy's urging, socially minded Jewish leaders like Jacob Schiff were appearing at the HSGS annual meetings and wondering aloud *why* they had never been invited before.

The new president early persuaded copper magnate Leonard Lewisohn to join the board as treasurer. The fifteen lady managers gratefully retired to positions as "honorary directresses." And an all-male enlarged board of business leaders and professional men took their place. Soon a drive was under way to enroll 1500 subscribers at $10 per year, and Lewisohns, Warburgs, Loebs, and Schiffs were inscribing their names in the leather-bound register of contributors to a building fund.

After Leonard Lewisohn's death in 1901, his younger brother and partner, Adolph, agreed to serve as president of the society, while Levy stepped down to executive vice-president. The lawyer's choice of the German-born industrialist and mining tycoon to head the HSGS proved to be a brilliant one.

Adolph Lewisohn, who lost his own mother when he was six, maintained a lifelong interest in orphaned and dependent children. In his unpublished autobiography, he has described having to trudge alone to the synagogue every day for the year following his mother's death. There, every day, he would recite the *kaddish,* the orphan's prayer. He remembered, too, the long lines of orphans passing in the streets of Hamburg. Each child carried a little cup on the end of a stick into which passersby — including more afflu-ent little boys like Adolph Lewisohn — could drop coins. Even then, to him, it did not seem "the right way to treat such little children."

Unlike most uptown Jews, the new president of the HSGS actually had *seen* how the children of the Lower East Side lived. He had often accompanied his elderly friend, Seligman Solomon, on the HOA trustee's regular round, investigating needy families. He knew the feel of the tenements on Broome and Hester and Ludlow Streets, and the look of the littered streets crowded with people.

Most important of all for the president of a child care organi-zation, Adolph Lewisohn had a great respect for professionals and a great willingness to consult with them.

The lives of the children at the HSGS really began to change in 1903 when a 27-year old high school teacher of German called Ludwig B. Bernstein was appointed superintendent. It was then that the children began referring to the new administration as the "Kindly Rebels."

Dr. Bernstein did not at all like what he found at the HSGS. As he wrote five years later: "It was neither the much advertised horrible check apron, nor the terrible bell, nor the institution oil-cloth in the dining room that caused me to look around for ways and means how to avoid institutionalism. They appeal to the su-perficial and sentimental observer but they do not strike at the root of the thing. I felt very much more concerned about the character of the relations between the adults and the children. . . . The relations were official, nothing more or less. The supervisors were strict disciplinarians and disciplinarians only, and the children were judged solely from the point of view of their conduct as affecting institution rules and institution routine."

"A genuine pioneer with something of the fervor of the old prophets," "an educator to the depths of his heart." This was how a former HSGS ward, Michael Sharlitt, later described Dr. Bernstein. The educator's fervor apparently was immediately challenged, and the new superintendent turned to the "glorious work of individualizing children."

But how could he change attitudes so entrenched?

"At first, by way of experiment, a few clubs for the younger children were introduced, the club leaders being experienced kindergarten teachers who devoted a few evenings a week to songs, games and chats with our children." But the poorly trained supervisors complained loudly at having their cast-iron routines disrupted. They protested that the smaller children were overstimulated by these new activities and later disturbed the older children with their noise.

"The grave nature of this complaint," however, did not prevent Dr. Bernstein from noticing that the little ones seemed fairly bursting with joy. "The possibility of communicating to their club leaders all their little childish troubles, worries, and joys had almost revolutionized them. They fairly mobbed the superintendent in an attempt to tell him of the glorious times they had spent."

Supervisory frowns notwithstanding, additional clubs were started with the help of the two new alumni associations and some of the trustees' children. Now the accusations changed to "sowing seeds of discontent" among the children. Oh, worse! The outsiders were beginning to "know too much about the institution."

In time, objections subsided. Several supervisors even became club leaders. By 1908, the orphanage had 43 different social and cultural groups, with its senior club a daring mixture of boys and girls.

Dr. Bernstein was not through shocking the disciplinarians. What, he asked, was the single thing most responsible for the sameness of action and appearance always remarked among institutional children? The monitorial system with its rigid military methods of maintaining order, of course. "One, jacket off. Two, sit down. Three, right shoe off. Four, left shoe off. Five, right stocking. . . ." And so on. *That* was the life of an orphan.

With one stroke Bernstein abolished the monitors. In their place he set up two self-governing Republics. One was for boys, one for girls. All officers were to be elected by the children themselves.

Such a plan worked well at the small George Junior Republic in Ithaca. But could a huge orphanage introduce so much democracy? Surely the dignity of the institution would crumble and anarchy would take over.

No such thing happened. Soon management, supervisors, and children were working together in astonishing harmony.

The Republics not only governed the institution. They also managed a savings bank; ran a coop store that sold candy, stationery and toys, and whose profits provided spending money to the poorest wards; and handled the fast-growing institutional library. An exuberant attempt to dictate the orphanage menu however appears to have been hastily crushed.

The day-to-day life of the girls also took an abrupt turn for the better in 1903 when Sara Canter came from the Educational Alliance to become HSGS matron. The rapture with which the girls greeted the housekeeping training she introduced was one measure of the emptiness of their previous life. "We had no way of knowing these things in an existence completely detached from the rest of the world," wrote Amelia Davis. In addition, more qualified supervisors "of our own faith" were hired, Miss Davis recalled.

Professionalization made a small beginning at the HSGS in 1902 when the first salaried admissions officer was hired to do the work formerly done by members of the board. In addition to investigating all applications —" in order to get a clear picture of the child's past and thus . . . find ourselves in possession of the key to his present and future treatment"— Jacob Barshein was "to keep a constant survey of the circumstances of parents and relations of our wards," with a view to shortening the child's stay in the overcrowded institution.

But there was also a perceptible shift in *attitude* toward parents. They were more welcome to visit now. Dr. Bernstein even conducted parent meetings! The children were encouraged to write home and not to be ashamed to address their parents in Yiddish. When necessary even an interpreter (!) was provided.

The HSGS also was beginning to extend its responsibility past the child's discharge. In 1898, Leonard Lewisohn had endowed the first HSGS scholarship. Another Lewisohn gift provided $5,000 for a "Discharged Children's Fund" to help children leaving the institution get a start in life. The HOA already had far larger endowments for both purposes.

But was it not also important to know what happened *afterwards?* The first follow-up study was conducted, on his own time, by Jacob Barshein in 1902. The admissions officer moved discreetly. He was careful not to contact the more successful alumni at their place of business for fear of embarrassing them by exposing their past.

In 1908, the HSGS appointed the popular Louis J. Cohen head of a new "Aftercare Department." He was to "follow up the occupations and living conditions of our Alumni, assist them in securing positions, and keep in touch with the firms with whom our alumni are employed." It was again a recognition that full-time professional employees were needed in work formerly done — often haphazardly — by volunteers. But the alumni themselves were among the strongest supporters of the aftercare work, then as later. Members of the Young Folks Fraternal League, founded in 1902, and the Leonard Lewisohn Club, founded three years later, often provided loans or other kinds of assistance for their fellows.

Naturally, quarantines intruded on everyone's plans. Levy had not been at the HSGS long when the Board of Health closed it for 40 days for measles. The next year the children lost twelve weeks of school because of scarlet fever. Levy seized the bull by the horns and persuaded the city to build a special annex to the school where the children could continue to attend separate classes, even though quarantined. Iron doors through which no germ could pass separated the two units.

But it was the famous battle with ringworm of the scalp in 1902 that really challenged the HSGS resourcefulness and caused a drastic shakeup of the medical department. The annual report describes the strenuous measures adopted to stamp out this tenacious infection.

The orphanage was closed, all new arrivals cancelled and a special bacteriological lab set up. An eminent dermatologist was hastily summoned to direct treatment and a large staff of nurses and attendants engaged. No longer needed for new arrivals, a recently rented reception house was turned into a medical annex and a large private house a few blocks away leased as a hospital facility for the boys. On February 6, the first 140 girls were sent to Lebanon Hospital. Not until August 21 was the last one returned to her dormitory.

Altogether 450 children were affected. They had lost a full term of school, and the resources of the institution had been strained to near breaking point. The report to the board commented unhappily: "The key to the difficulty really lies in our overcrowded condition." With facilities for 750, the HSGS orphanage had 922 children at the time of the outbreak.

"Of course," continued the report, "we could have avoided the tremendous expense for the care of these sick children and the worriment and care . . . by turning them over to the public authorities who would have transferred them to Randall's Island. But we felt that the children required more than ever our parental care and we were unwilling to have these children cared for in any other than a Jewish home."

There were not only religious reasons for this reluctance. With the inferior care offered in the public hospitals, children sometimes were confined to ringworm wards for three to five *years* before the infection was cured. The indifferent schooling provided in such places could handicap a child for life. The child never again caught up. The HSGS had done its best to avoid any such educational impairment on this occasion, even hiring special teachers to help its children keep up their studies.

But the die was cast. Levy called in an energetic young resident from Mount Sinai to serve as attending physician and overhaul the HSGS medical program. So efficient were Dr. Milton A. Gershel's methods that although scarlet fever, diptheria and typhoid all broke out in the asylum in 1905, each was confined to a single case.

For the first time, the children had their heights and weights recorded and scientifically compared with children living elsewhere. As expected! The HSGS ward was well below average size at the most crucial growing period of a child's life.

The problem could hardly be blamed on the orphanage. Twenty percent of its children were there because of TB in one or both parents, ten percent because of parental insanity, and 23% because their parents had been removed to some "unknown" hospital due to chronic illness such as asthma. In short, more than half came from homes that were not only poor but also undermined by long-term illness. Was it any wonder if a child's growth was stunted or if some had learning problems in school?

But the Kindly Rebels saw it as their responsibility to overcome their children's handicaps. New arrivals now were given an enriched diet; and the most delicate received a special diet the year around. An honest attempt also was made to vary the dreary institutional menu that induced so many underweight children to hide food in the hollow places under the long dining tables.

From the start nothing had been so clear to Levy as the fact that the "glorious work of individualizing children" would require far more than the sum of all the reforms that possibly could be introduced into the cramped congregate institution. The HSGS needed a new building. But it must be a building that would make it possible to truly revolutionize the lives of its children.

On a trip to England, the young lawyer had been greatly impressed by an institution called Barkenside. It was one of the first children's institution to be built on the cottage plan. The youngsters lived in groups of 25 or so, in small, separate cottages, each headed by a motherly woman. It seemed to him that no child in that institution was lost in the mass. The house mother had time to notice and listen to even the smallest and shyest of her brood.

For years, partisans of foster home care had pointed to the greater independence and self-confidence of a child brought up in a family, and its greater ability to relate to another human being. The defenders of institutions pointed, with equal conviction, to the abuses so often suffered by children placed in the poorly supervised foster homes of that day.

True, an "act to prevent evils and abuses in connection with placing out of children" had been passed in 1898. But the files of the SPCC were still full of tales of children beaten, starved, worked half to death, sexually molested. How much simpler to watch over 700 to 1,000 children all living together than to attempt to supervise the same number scattered in countless separate homes!

But the cottage plan seemed to combine the best features of both congregate and family care — the safety of the institution with the intimacy and individual attention only possible in a home. The New York Orphanage, headed by Dr. Rex Reeder, already had converted to this plan.

Levy's enthusiasm for Barkenside proved persuasive to his board. With Joseph L. Buttenweiser as chairman, a building committee soon was canvassing the city for a plot of land large enough for the HSGS plan. Not only ample room for buildings and playgrounds would be necessary; the new institution also was to have its own school, including for the first time at the HSGS a broad technical training program. 150 different locations were scanned before the men finally settled on 175 rolling acres of fields and woods near the village of Pleasantville in Westchester County.

President Lewisohn began organizing conferences of child welfare experts to discuss possible programs and plans for the new institution, while Ludwig Bernstein sailed away to Germany and England to study the latest European teaching methods. The superintendent came back with a satchel full of sample curricula and a tentative plan for the board's approval. Ten times the plan was discussed, and revised, before all were satisfied.

But while these intramural preparations engrossed the HSGS, there was no let-up in the waves of immigration pounding the walls outside. Refugees were landing at the rate of 90,000 a year and families continued to break apart.

Back in 1901, Jacob Schiff already had reminded the board that 25% of all inmates of juvenile reformatories now were Jewish as against a Jewish population of only 19%. Most of these children of course were not "criminals" but little vagrants "without visible means of support." But to the traditionally law-abiding Jewish community, such figures were shocking. They were also a direct reflection of the extreme poverty of the Jewish immigrant group.

"I don't believe it is fully understood," insisted Schiff, "that this institution stands between Jewish honor and Jewish shame." Had not the HSGS been founded to care for just such children?

At the next year's annual meeting, Levy appealed to his audience to ". . . let the Jewish public of America know that annually 200 of its helpless innocent youths are shut out from Judaism because of the narrowness of our means and through their apathy. Talk of this at all times and let its shameful significance sink into the public Jewish conscience."

Such rhetoric served to prime the fund-raising drive for the new building, but the situation was indeed serious and growing worse. By 1904, 750 Jewish children were in Catholic, Protestant and city institutions.

Three years later the BHOA, which had been coping fairly well with its local population growth, was swamped as immigrants began to bypass the crowded Lower East Side and look for homes across the East River. The Brooklyn board bemoaned the "influence of the (new) Williamsburg Bridge" which with two roadways, two sidewalks, and six tracks for surface and elevated cars was proving a godsend "for Manhattan's needy who cross the bridge in hordes in search of less congestion and lower cost of living."

With only 300 beds, the BHOA was planning a wing for 200 more. Two hundred Brooklyn children were in the HSGS. Hundreds of others were scattered in 15 non-Jewish institutions. Applicants with skin diseases now were left to the tender mercies of the public ringworm wards.

The prospect of perhaps 1,000 dependent Jewish children being forced into Christian families or Christian institutions for lack of facilities of their own faith once again proved too much. Despite their distrust of the whole concept of foster home care, more and more often the solution entered in the admission books next to the young applicant's name came to be "boarded."

Traditionally, "boarding-out" a child had been a last resort for the Jewish institutions — a purely temporary measure to prevent over-crowding, or a way to dispose of a sickly, handicapped or unmanageable child difficult to include in the regimented institutional life. Now it seemed it might be necessary to regard it as a routine way to care for many children.

In 1904, the first joint formal steps were taken to meet the accelerating crisis. The three great orphanages joined with the Hebrew Infants Asylum, the new Jewish Protectory and Aid Society (now the Hawthorne Cedar Knolls School of the Jewish Board of Guardians), and the United Hebrew Charities to form a "Bureau of Boarding and Placing-Out Jewish Dependent Children."

The city's Department of Charities appointed a special Examiner of Dependent Children, "to endeavor to find satisfactory homes in Jewish families, either for adoption or with temporary payment for board." The city subsidy was the same as for institutional care — $110 per year per child. Advertisements for homes were placed in Jewish papers and notices were posted in public places throughout the country. Some of the 146 homes applying proved difficult for the local inspector to check. They were as far away as Alaska, North Dakota, Michigan, Canada and Alabama.

With Dr. Bernstein as director, Dr. Gershel as physician, Jacob Barshein as "inspector and organizer of local committees," a Miss A. Wolf as "visitor," one trained nurse, a *mohel* to perform circumcisions, one stenographer, and a ladies committee led by Hannah B. Einstein, the new bureau during its first four years managed to place 1,000 children. Mrs. Einstein's committee provided clothing and also helped visit homes.

When the cooperative arrangement between the institutions collapsed after one year, the bureau became a permanent part of the HSGS, while the others set up their own boarding departments.

For the most part the children boarded under this formal plan were still those least adaptable to institutional life, although a healthy full orphan could be placed on trial with a family anxious to adopt. (This had long been a practice of the orphanages.) In 1907, Dr. Bernstein also transferred all the HSGS "babies" — the children between three and six — to the Boarding-Out Bureau. The superintendent had become convinced that for these little ones a boarding home was not only "as good as" but, in fact, "much better than" a congregate institution. It was an enlightened viewpoint, not shared for many years by the Jewish community as a whole.

But even those who initially fought the boarding-out program could not help but be gratified to discover how many of the two- and three-year-old boys required circumcision — indisputable proof of timely rescue from Christian hands.

It was equally reassuring to receive letters of thanks from grateful parents who had visited their children in their new homes and were well pleased. Less welcome was the storm raised by the respected head of the Jewish Orphans' Home of Cleveland, Rabbi Wolfenstein, who insisted on paying surprise calls to several HOA foster homes at seven in the morning. (He had obtained 116 addresses through the HOA superintendent who certainly did not expect such early visits.) The Cleveland orphanage head's stated intent was to prove unequivocally that *no* home could possibly equal the orderly character-building routine of a congregate institution at the same hour. He later described his findings as "depressing in the extreme."

Foster home care might be viewed as a last resort by the Jewish institutional boards. But the idea of subsidizing a widowed mother to allow her to keep her children at home had always found favor. For years, first the synagogues, then the Hebrew Benevolent Society, the HOA and the United Hebrew Charities had included among their functions that of helping "respectable" widows with children hold their homes together. From the founding of the United Hebrew Charities in 1873 until 1907, the HOA had contributed $30,000 yearly to the Charities for this purpose. Since that time it had subsidized widows on its own.

These were private funds, however. By 1907, such funds were only a drop in a huge bucket of crushing human need. The HOA had almost nine half-orphans for every full orphan. The HSGS had five to one. The Brooklyn orphanage, 14 to one. The Hebrew Infants Asylum had ten half orphans for every child with no parents. Some children had a father left rather than a mother, of course. But too many had mothers who were "sick and unable to work" in large part because of their anxious struggle to hold their homes together.

The curious fact was that the city would subsidize a boarding home or an institution to care for a widow's child, but would not give the same money to the child's own mother to care for it at home. There were no public funds to help widows.

Hannah B. Einstein, who headed the ladies committee of the HSGS' Boarding and Placing Out Bureau, was one who felt that more should be done for widowed mothers. Those who shared her concern were greatly cheered by a historic meeting of child welfare experts held at the White House in 1909.

The conference — the first White House Conference on the Care of Dependent Children — dealt a severe blow to the institutions of the day by voting overwhelmingly in favor of family care. "Home life is the highest and finest product of civilization," read the conference's final statement. "Such aid . . . as may be necessary to maintain suitable homes for the rearing of the children" should be given whenever possible, rather than uprooting a child from its natural home.

If the home could not be saved, continued the report, a foster home should be provided. Only as a last resort and in special cases should a child be institutionalized and then only in an institution built on the cottage plan.

The conference, sponsored by President Theodore Roosevelt, heard a paper by the HSGS president, Adolph Lewisohn, on the subject of pensions for widows. The experts were not urging public funds for this purpose. They agreed that private funds were better. Public relief tended to be at a starvation level. It was felt that it often harmed more than it helped and could be demoralizing to a family. But the principle had been firmly acknowledged: when possible, the home should be kept intact.

In New York, Hannah Einstein founded the Widowed Mothers' Fund Association to raise money to help needy widows. She soon realized, however, that one more source of private money would not solve the vast problem. There were just too many widowed mothers.

The HOA superintendent, Solomon Loewenstein, arrived at the same conclusion when he carried out a study of fatherless families aided by Jewish agencies. He found the families he investigated living in congested apartments, barely able to keep alive on the small sums handed out to them. One agency gave a family $10 for rent, another gave it $8 for food. Not even an efficiency expert could have fitted the pieces together, and managed to survive.

The Cleveland orphanage head referred to earlier also visited some widowed mothers. He found their situation heartbreaking: ". . . such trying scenes I have not witnessed since . . . 1866 . . . when I, as Rabbi of Insterberg visited the Russian cities, Kovno and Wilma . . . where typhus and famine had been spreading. It is beyond my understanding how such squalor, such unsanitary conditions, should be permitted to exist in our country?" He felt at least ten more orphan asylums should be opened in New York to correct this intolerable situation.

But others were convinced that public funds to help hold the home together were the only answer. Mrs. Einstein joined with others like the reporter Sophie Irene Loeb and Florence Kelley of the National Consumers League in a struggle to persuade the New York State legislature to pass a law to pay pensions to widows.

The law was passed in 1915. Known as the "Child Welfare Act," it required every county to set up a child welfare board with authority to grant allowances to widowed mothers with children under 16. The allowances were small — an average of $7.99 monthly per child at first. Yet within two years New York City had 3,000 fewer children in its orphanages. The missing children were living at home with their mothers. (The HOA continued to contribute occasional supplementary funds. In 1916 it assisted 161 widowed mothers.)

Meanwhile, at the HSGS, plans were proceeding briskly for the move to Pleasantville — despite the fears of some who warned of the "destructiveness of Jewish children" and strongly doubted the wisdom of "surrounding the children of the poor with what appeared to be a relatively comfortable mode of life." Advertisements for house mothers had been placed in the Anglo-Jewish press and broadcast throughout the country.

Replies flooded in. It took a year to sift the 150 applications received, interview the women, and select the 25 best prospects. No specific academic requirements were set. To Dr. Bernstein the woman's character, personality, maturity, housekeeping skill, her interest in and previous experience with children, and her ability to perform all domestic religious rites were all-important.

Among those first housemothers were a cousin of United States Supreme Court Justice Louis Brandeis, the sister of a famous American painter, a Mielziner of the stage-designing family, and a young woman named Mary Boretz who would become one of the great pioneers in the field of foster home care.

Eleven months before the move to the country, 300 of the older children were taken out of the public school and put into a special educational program similar to the one they would find in the new cottage institution. They found themselves taking shop and needlecraft classes now in addition to the usual academic subjects. Gone were the black suits and smocks of the "crows" and "ravens", as the girls and boys used to call each other. They were replaced by better and more varied clothing. Football, basketball and handball were introduced and there were regular trips to vaudeville and motion picture theaters.

In preparation for life in the new cottages, boys as well as girls now were taught to cook and began practising tentative domestic routines. Would it be better to have separate cottage kitchens or one central kitchen? Should maids and handymen be employed or could the children do the housekeeping? The actual completion of the architectural plan for the new institution awaited the outcome of this experimentation. The cottage mothers made last minute suggestions for changes, and the final routines were endlessly rehearsed.

All this was necessary to avoid too abrupt a change from the old style of life to the new. The fear was that sudden change could complicate adjustment for years to come.

There would be room for only 500 children in the 25 cottages already completed. Many of the older ones could be discharged, of course. But 100 others, including all the 7-year-olds, were placed in boarding homes. The new institution would take no children younger than 8.

Came the great day? July 1, 1912. Four hundred and eighty boys and girls lined up outside the old building on 150th Street, waving little American flags and sneaking excited glances at the cottage numbers pinned to their garments. Traffic was rerouted as they marched — in cottage formation, stepping smartly to the music of their band — down Broadway and toward the HOA.

There, behind the enormous orphan city, the column halted. For there, "loyal to their sister Home were the children, many feet deep, watching, and some weeping." The HOA band played a last farewell, and the little flags of the HSGS children waved on, down Broadway and across 125th Street to the New York Central Railroad.

# Chapter 4

# Exploring New Territory

*"But the sight we liked best was that of our Cottage Mothers who had come down to greet us. They, too, had their Cottage numbers pinned to their dresses so that we'd know our mothers and they their children. And so up the hill we went with our mothers— toward Home."* H.B.C. IN H.S.G.S. CAVALCADE—1879-1940.

**M**OST OF THE 480 CHILDREN who made the 30-mile trip to Pleasantville that first day of July, had never before seen the rolling fields and forests of open country. And as for the buildings! A lawyer recalled in 1963, "We were like bugs flying all over. We ran in and out of all the cottages. We chased each other across the square. We climbed inside the huge ice boxes which looked bigger than a whole East Side apartment. We got inside the furnaces. We jumped on the beds and flushed the toilets. We were explorers in a new world." Despite all the preparations of the preceding year, it took months to settle down.

Not only the children were excited by the new cottage institution. In 1912, the director of the Child Helping Department of the Russell Sage Foundation described it as "undoubtedly the best equipped institution for children in the world." Child care workers from Europe and America came to study it. Within five years, three new institutions were constructed on its precise pattern. Harvard University requested a special display of pictures and charts describing the institution and its program. It wanted this for a permanent exhibit in the University's Social Ethics Museum.

Even the President of the United States, William Howard Taft, found time to view the Pleasantville campus while on a visit to Adolph Lewisohn's nearby home. When Taft left he was wearing the gold button seal of the Boys' and Girls' Republics.

The focus of the program arousing all this interest was the cottage and the classroom — with the cottage mother and her influence at the heart of the plan.

Each cottage was home for the 25 to 30 boys or girls who ate, slept and studied there. Ages — but not sexes! — were mixed within a cottage. Big Brothers and Big Sisters helped their Little Brothers and Little Sisters, tucked them in at night, made sure their beds were properly assembled in the morning. The children did all their own housekeeping — sweeping, dusting, scrubbing the floors — and helped their "mothers" prepare the strictly kosher meals.

To be sure neatness had been easier to maintain under the old system. (As Dr. Bernstein remarked later, the best cottage mothers were rarely the most meticulous housekeepers.) But the superintendent's standards were exacting, and the weekly intercottage contests for "the banner of cleanliness," "the banner of efficiency," and "the banner of personal appearance" appealed to cottage loyalties.

Cottage Councils now reinforced the Republics. Visitors guided around campus by the eager children frequently remarked a democratic atmosphere unknown in other congregate institutions.

But it was the school part of the Pleasantville program that aroused the most intense professional interest. Leading educators here and abroad universally hailed it as "pioneering" and "a radical advance in progressive education."

The plan provided for three kinds of education combined into one interrelated curriculum. The academic studies included the usual math, history, English and science, but German, French and Latin also were compulsory for all children. Hebrew and Jewish history were taught as regular classroom subjects. But the most innovative feature was the vocational education program. This was designed to start with the first year of school and continue, along with the academic and religious subjects, until the final year which was to be a year of specialization in one or another technical field.

The curriculum of the technical school was impressive. Boys were offered woodwork, machine shop, electric shop, mechanical and free hand drawing, sheet metal, metal springs, and printing. Girls were firmly steered toward the garment trades, the kitchen and the business office. They could take plain sewing, dressmaking, costume designing, millinery, and embroidering, as well as domestic science, free-hand drawing, stenography and typewriting. Such a "sexist" division of vocational choices would earn the school sharp criticism from young women today. But it provided skills that were saleable in the job market of that day. "Radiotelegraphy and telephony" were later added for both sexes.

One unusual aspect of the intensive educational program was that it covered twelve years of school in only nine years. This it accomplished by cutting out all but a few weeks of the summer vacation and stretching the school day to seven and a half rather than the usual five hours. Every child was expected to finish high school before his discharge.

Despite its unorthodox features, the secondary school curriculum was officially approved by the Deputy Commissioner of the New York State Department of Education in 1915. It was the first time that the state had officially recognized a secondary school program which did not require 12 years of attendance, and the first time that any orphanage school had received equal rating with the regular public schools.

The technical program also earned unequivocal praise in 1914 from the Director of Industrial Arts of Columbia's Teachers College who found children 12 to 16 doing work he felt would easily compare with that done by 16 to 18 year olds elsewhere.

The challenging school naturally attracted talented young teachers. Foremost among these was its principal, Michael Sharlitt. A former ward of the old HSGS orphanage at 150th Street, Sharlitt had been the recipient of the first Samuel Lewisohn scholarship donated by Leonard Lewisohn in memory of his son in 1898. Years later, Sharlitt became the director of the Jewish Orphan's Home in Cleveland and helped transform that old congregate institution into the outstanding cottage plan residential treatment center called Bellefaire.

The versatile head of the technical program was Samuel Solender, who later became executive director of the Washington Heights and Inwood Branch of the Young Men's and Young Women's Hebrew Association. His son, Sanford Solender, is the present executive head of New York's Federation of Jewish Philanthropies.

But the move to the country with children who came from the most congested wards of the city and must one day be returned there highlighted problems long dormant under the surface of the old institutional life.

One was the problem of the return home. The Kindly Rebels' budding attempts to narrow the gulf between the wards of the huge uptown German-run institution and their orthodox Eastern European immigrant parents on the Lower East Side had been further complicated by the move. But many Lower East Side Jews had long felt, in any case, it would be far better to keep the children in the old neighborhood than to send them to the HOA and the HSGS where they could only learn to be ashamed of their origins.

In 1914, a group of Roumanian Jews on the Lower East Side scraped up enough money from their impecunious neighbors to open an orthodox home for 20 boys in a remodeled brownstone at 39 East 7th Street. Only boys six to 13 were admitted to the Hebrew National Orphan Home as it later was called. Girls were more readily taken in by relatives and, anyhow, they were considered less in need of the orthodox training offered in the new institution.

Three years later, to meet the urgent wartime need of orphaned babies under 6, Galician Jews opened the Israel Orphan Asylum in a new six-story white brick building attached to a former Methodist Church on East Second Street between Avenues C and D. The asylum opened in a whirl of patriotic bunting, with the streets filled with children marching behind a band. Judge Gustave Hartman, an East Side boy himself, largely financed out of his own pocket the effort to found the home.

Despite their neighborhood origins, both orthodox orphanages soon loosened their ties to the Lower East Side. The HNOH moved to a 22-acre property in Yonkers in 1922, while the IOA bought a large summer home in Far Rockaway in 1923. But the two remained closely connected. IOA boys were transferred to the HNOH when they reached six years, leaving the girls with the younger children.

In the meantime, it was becoming increasingly clear both to the HSGS alumni and to Pleasantville club leaders that far more needed to be done for children who would be released in the future than ever had been done for those discharged in the past.

At an alumni reunion, those present passed a "solemn resolution" that work along these lines must start at once. More important to future progress than any mere resolution was the fact that a tactful and determined young woman, Alice S. Seligsberg, accepted a unanimous draft to serve as president of an organization which had not, as yet, been founded.

Alice Seligsberg was the director of club activities at the HSGS and the daughter of the society's second vice-president, Louis Seligsberg. She and the friends she gathered for the purpose boldly mapped out an aftercare program for future graduates. When the board refused their request for funds, they promptly formed an independent agency, named it Fellowship House, and with the help of several board members, raised a modest first year's budget of $2,500.

The Pleasantville institution agreed to pay for specific services to its alumni; Dr. Bernstein was to be a member of the aftercare agency's board. But Pleasantville was to have no control over the policies of Fellowship House. This independence, in later years, proved to be the aftercare agency's greatest source of creative strength.

In January, 1913, Fellowship House hired its first worker and set up shop in two rooms on West 124th Street. Its plan was simple. Former wards would find here 1) a place to meet; 2) one-to-one relationships with responsible adult "friends" to help tide them over their first difficult years of adjustment; 3) a free employment service; and 4) a homefinding bureau for those who had no place to go on discharge. Soon it was found necessary also to extend small loans. Payment for several weeks' board was made available to newly discharged boys. The girl without family or funds usually was placed in an "opportunity home" where she helped the woman of the house in exchange for her board, while attending school or working outside.

Fellowship House's homefinding bureau meticulously investigated and supervised the boarding homes and service homes it offered the children. Were the sleeping arrangements adequate? Was there sufficient privacy? What about food? The shy, inexperienced young person so recently returned to the big city was not left to bargain alone for essential rights.

Beyond these basic programs, plans were flexible. First, see what was needed. Then, try to provide it.

Within ten months, Fellowship House's first small office was overflowing. Boys were forced to meet on the stairs, in the halls, on the sidewalks outside. The agency moved in October, 1913, to a house at 32 West 115th Street.

Criticism of the new aftercare work was not long in coming. Why provide a gathering place and recreational activities? Wouldn't it be better for the children to attend the settlement houses? No, replied Miss Seligsberg, they need their own place to meet their old orphanage friends. The staff and board knew that the discharged children were shy of mixing old friends with new. They did not want people to know they came from an orphanage, for fear that might provoke pity. As one girl put it: "Once I get to be a success, then I'll let them know about the HSGS."

But why an employment service? inquired the critics. Wasn't that also encouraging dependence? Fellowship House pointed to the long waiting lists at the regular agencies. "Our children have no resources to fall back on and must have jobs right away."

Fellowship House could learn only from experience — "the steps and missteps taken on the way to the goal," as Alice Seligsberg put it. There was no precedent to go by.

It soon grew apparent that many of the young people in aftercare needed more than a volunteer "friend" to help them in their adjustment to the city.

As Fellowship House's executive director, Jacob Kepecs, said a few years later: "Independence usually comes gradually. And yet the children from the institution who have been more dependent during their stay there than ordinary children in their own homes, are expected to transform themselves from an utter state of dependency to a condition of complete independence — and all in one day."

Some children came with problems that should have been worked out in the institution, but weren't. They needed professional counseling. And what about the children who never came in? The younger ones released to their families, or the older ones too shy or perhaps too troubled to find their way to Fellowship House? Shouldn't these, too, be followed up?

The Department of Public Welfare was ready to pay $2.50 per year for three years for each child visited by a Fellowship House worker. But neither staff nor board felt this meager offer should be accepted.

For one thing, the Department required only a single visit a year. What genuine service could be provided in a single yearly visit? Wouldn't the arrangement merely build the temptation to keep children on the rolls while paying only perfunctory home visits?

There seemed to be only one way to find out. Dr. Bernstein agreed to lend Fellowship House one of the Pleasantville cottage mothers, Mary Boretz, to conduct a two-month trial study. Her report convinced the aftercare agency's board that a follow-up of every child discharged was essential. The report was equally emphatic that a single yearly visit was utterly inadequate. *Every* child needed several visits a year, and *every* visit must be seen as an opportunity to provide service to both child and family.

It also was agreed that every home must be visited *before* the child's discharge from the institution or boarding home. How else avoid the kinds of situations that Mary Boretz found? The child sent home to a tubercular father and a mentally disturbed mother who had just been released after seven years in the city hospital. The little boy sent home only because an older brother or sister had reached working age — although any caller could plainly see that his mother was exhausted by years of trying to support the children left at home and now desperately needed a breathing spell. Was it fair to expect a father, earning very little money and heavily in debt for the care of his tubercular wife, to take on the added burden of a nine-year old bundle of mischief whom even the institution had found hard to handle?

Fellowship House accepted the Department of Public Welfare's stipend. But it set its own standards, and it added Mary Boretz to its staff. The uncompromising young woman was to follow-up the younger children discharged to their homes. In order not to embarrass them, the older children would continue to be seen at Fellowship House, as before.

The agency never limited its aftercare to the three years paid for by Welfare. The free loans, job-finding help and counseling continued as long as a youngster needed them.

As time went on, follow-up observations led to some disconcerting conclusions. For every two or three children discharged from Pleasantville, another was discharged from the HSGS Boarding Bureau or sent from an HSGS foster home to Pleasantville. Now, what about these children? It became very apparent to the aftercare agency that youngsters who had passed through the boarding homes were far more deprived than those who had spent their years at the institution. Why should this be? Case after case was investigated, until Fellowship House realized that the Boarding Bureau was, in effect, still being used as a dumping ground for the institution.

Three kinds of children were boarded out. The first were never intended to reach Pleasantville. They were children with physical or mental defects that would make them difficult to care for at the institution. The second was the child for whom there was at the moment no available bed. And the third was the little one between five and eight years old — too old for the Home for Hebrew Infants (formerly the Hebrew Infants Asylum) but still too young for the cottages.

When a bed was ready or a child reached its eighth birthday, the children "okay for Pleasantville" were taken from the boarding home without warning and sent to the institution. It made no difference how happy that child might have been in that home. Off he or she went.

Later, Mary Boretz wrote: "Two years of watching this process of child going from (the infants asylum) to boarding home to institution, made those of us who were watching it very disturbed. A child apparently absorbed into a family was one day notified to come to the office for an examination, and never returned to his classmates, his friends on the block. In no way was he consulted on this important decision and disposition of himself. As one foster mother said, 'When I kissed the children goodnight I never knew but that the morning mail would bring a letter notifying me that they would not be mine any longer'."

It wasn't that the boarding homes were not supervised. They

were. But supervision meant only a monthly visit to make certain the children were healthy, and sometimes a surprise visit in the middle of the night to check on sleeping accommodations. Heights and weights were taken, a trained nurse came when they were sick, and a doctor when they were sicker. But at no point were the emotional needs of the children considered. The policy was one unthinkingly inherited from the past. Even the boarding rate had not changed in fourteen years. It was still pegged at two dollars a week, in contrast to the six dollar rate paid for aftercare homes by Fellowship House.

In 1918, Fellowship House submitted its report to the board of the HSGS. The all-male board was sincerely shocked at the injustice done the children. It promptly severed the Bureau's dependence on Pleasantville and appointed Mary Boretz to replace Jacob Barshein who had been in charge from the Bureau's first days.

The concerned gentlemen of the HSGS board further decided they needed women in their own ranks. They invited Adolph Lewisohn's daughter, Mrs. Arthur Lehman, and Mrs. Sylvan Stix to become trustees. The Boarding Bureau Committee, which likewise had been composed only of men, was swept clean, reorganized and given almost autonomous powers. The new committee included both HSGS vice-presidents, Samuel Levy and Louis Seligsberg; a future New York State governor, Herbert H. Lehman; Mrs. Stix, and Mrs. Arthur Lehman. Because she was a mother, Mrs. Stix was made chairwoman.

The directive from the board to the committee was explicit: "No child who is happily placed in a home shall be removed."

For many years, Fellowship House continued its role of gadfly to the HSGS and to the Department of Public Welfare. Its preliminary investigations of homes at first caused as many as one-third of the discharges ordered by the city to be cancelled or postponed — until a family could be helped to make plans for reabsorbing the child or arrangements made for the child elsewhere.

But now more and more the staff became preoccupied with another question: the difficulties involved in reuniting families separated for so many years. Often, they discovered, adjustment proved impossible and the child had to move into a boarding home.

Wouldn't more work with the family during the years in place-ment, more frequent visits home, more preparation before dis-charge — wouldn't all these have eased the final reunion? Might not more preliminary work shorten the very *time* of separation? Surrendering a child to an institution or a boarding home fre-quently demoralized a family so that they hesitated to claim it once again even when they could have done so. A family had to be helped to see that the medical care and education provided by the institution were not more important than what the family itself could offer its child.

And what about those cases where placement could have been avoided altogether if other kinds of help had been available? Thanks to the law passed in 1914, a widow now could obtain public relief to help hold her home together. But not every poverty-stricken mother was a widow. Some had unemployed or sick husbands. Others had never been married. No public funds were available to these.

More and more the staff of Fellowship House came to feel that too often its task was the reconstruction of lives that need not have been disrupted in the first place. In 1918, its new ex-ecutive director, Jacob Kepecs, expressed the agency's emerging point of view. "Our immediate object," he said, "is to deal objec-tively with effects or results. But our remoter aim must be to deal with causes."

Mr. Kepecs, who was the first professional social worker to head Fellowship House, stressed individual casework with children more, recreational activities less. The causes of a child's problem might lie with his family and the absence of the preventive measures that could have preserved it. But, once that damage was done, the road to a child's reconstruction was an individual road.

In that second decade of the twentieth century, other influences were also at work, slowly bending the direction of New York's Jewish child care agencies. Depressions, immediately preceding and following the war, and the needs of Jews overseas brought keen competition for the charitable funds of the Jewish community. Money was scarce. In 1917, after eight years of discussion, 24 Manhattan and Bronx agencies formed a Federation for the Sup-port of Jewish Philanthropic Societies in New York City. Among the charter members were the HOA, the HSGS, and the Home for Hebrew Infants. (Brooklyn Jews led by the BHOA, had formed the first such Federation in the country in 1910.) The new Federation was to discourage overlapping charities, handle fundraising, estimate the community's need, allocate money, and attempt to establish standards. It was a necessary step forward. Inevitably, it created pressures for change.

Although the orphanages retained their right to formulate their own policies, they had to give up the contributing members who had for so long helped them offer their children a level of care impossible on the city stipend alone. One of the first victims of the tight money situation was the widely admired educational program at Pleasantville.

The per capita cost of care for a child at the cottage institution in 1912 was $365 a year — twice the city's subsidy rate. Costs now were reduced by accepting more children and introducing various economies, but the problems of raising money during the war made the educational program appear an unnecessary luxury to some board members.

To aggravate the problem, a polio epidemic in 1918 forced the cancellation of admissions for that year. Empty beds proliferated. And those who always had been lukewarm about the idea of a private school for orphans had a point. The children discharged to their families before graduating from Pleasantville had a difficult time transferring to the radically different program of the city high schools. The board decided it would be not only less expensive, but also more realistic, to allow the city to take over the education of the Pleasantville children.

The decision was made in 1918. Dr. Bernstein resigned in protest. The day he left, the campus was in the middle of a quarantine. The superintendent walked from cottage to cottage saying his last goodbyes.

Early in 1919, Dr. Leon Goldrich, a Manhattan high school principal, was called in as director of the Pleasantville institution, and the school on campus became an annex of P. S. 42 in Manhattan.

One of the early problems facing the Child Care Committee of the new Federation was the eternal rivalry that existed between orphanages over children to fill beds. Most children reached the institutions via the Department of Public Welfare which was run by untrained appointees of the big political machine, Tammany Hall. (Although there were always some children — overage or otherwise not eligible by city standards — who were maintained on the institution's "free list," while others were partially paid for by relatives.)

The children sent by the city were haphazardly assigned. The department had a blackboard. On this it listed the names of the various orphanages and, next to each name, that day's tally of empty beds. If a child was under five and the Home for Hebrew Infants showed an empty space, away that child went to the HHI. If a child was over six, off to the HSGS or the HOA — whichever showed the most vacancies.

No one ever stopped to wonder which institution — or which form of placement — might be most helpful to which child. It was a matter of age, empty beds, and chance.

One of those most concerned about this inefficient and some-times unfeeling system for disposing of children was a 47-year-old Federation board member, Herman W. Block, who, in 1919, was made chairman of its Child Care Committee. Block was also chairman of the Administrative Committee of the Hebrew Shelter-ing Guardian Society and a member of its board.

Under his leadership the Bureau of Jewish Social Research was asked to make a survey of the Jewish child care situation in New York City. The report was blunt. It strongly urged a central clearing bureau for Jewish children as the only reasonable way out of total chaos.

Prodded by a perfectly timed request for such a bureau from the Commissioner of Public Welfare to Solomon Loewenstein — who had left the HOA to become executive director of Federa-tion — the reluctant Jewish institutions at last agreed. With funds from the Nathan Hofheimer Foundation, the Jewish Children's Clearing Bureau opened its first office in mid-1922 at 101 West 119 Street. Three years later it moved to a building at 1645 York Avenue donated by Mrs. Herbert R. Limburg (later Mrs. Jacob Scheuer) as a memorial to her parents.

On the new bureau's board sat both lay and professional

members of the ten Manhattan agencies it served, including the HOA, HSGS and HHI. It was the first time that Jewish philanthropic organizations in New York City had given professionals equal voice with laymen in hammering out policies.

Applications flooded in. Before the office could be equipped or the phone installed, there were 265 applications involving 483 children. By January of 1924, the Bureau, with a staff of 16 overworked people, had received 1,747 applications involving more than 3,000 children.

With Herman Block as president and his ally and friend, Alice Seligsberg, as executive director, it was clear from the beginning that the new agency would be no helpless pawn in the hands of the institutions. The presence on its board of representatives of the Child Adoption Committee of the Free Synagogue, the Home Bureau, the Widowed Mothers' Fund Association and the United Hebrew Charities — which by this time provided many family services — served as further guarantee.

The new agency was in a perfect position to influence change in child care practices. Not only was it required to study applications for placement and decide on the appropriate action; it also was to rule on applications for discharge and for transfer of children from one institution to another or from one program to another.

For the first time, there was enough staff and a large enough budget to permit a thorough investigation of applications and a careful study of each child's home — when there was a home — before reaching a decision for or against placement.

No longer was the first question: "*What* institution?" Now that question was: "Is placement *necessary?*"

From the first, the Clearing Bureau refused to regard destitution as in itself "sufficient cause" for removing a child from his family. If poverty was the chief problem, then it was a case not for institutions or boarding homes, but for the family-serving agencies who could help people in trouble obtain financial help or practical service. In other cases, temporary placement might be enough to tide a home over until a sick mother improved or a marital difficulty straightened out.

Under this policy, solutions other than long-term placement

were found for seventy-five percent of all applicants in the Bureau's first 18 months of work. Gone was the day when a Jewish child was shipped to a huge institution with little preliminary investigation. Gone was the day when the fate of a child was decided entirely by the number and location of empty beds.

But the most significant change in the child care picture was this: for the first time, foster homes were to be the placement of choice for the care of Jewish children between three and ten. In the battle of the institutions versus foster home care that would continue for another 16 years, Alice Seligsberg and Herman Block stood shoulder-to-shoulder on the side of the foster home. Nevertheless, the jockeying for children was not completely over.

# Chapter 5

# Institution or Foster Home?

*"We have a cottage institution for dependent children at Pleasantville that cost us a million dollars. But if it be proved that children can all be better cared for in some other way, I am willing to see it scrapped for their good."* ADOLPH LEWISOHN, QUOTED BY HENRY W. THURSTON.

T HE IDEA THAT foster home care is better than institutional care for children did not really start with Mary Boretz—effective though she was in crusading for it.

As far back as 1853, Charles Loring Brace of the Children's Aid Society was taking homeless children off the streets of New York and sending them out to live with families in the West. He claimed healthy, normal children had no need of institutional care. Within 25 years, his Society's bi-weekly caravans transported 48,000 children to new homes. But there was much justified criticism of this practice because foster homes so far away were virtually unsupervised, and children often mistreated. Still the concept had many defenders.

In 1866, Samuel Gridley Howe of the Massachusetts State Board of Charities expressed beliefs very similar to those Mary Boretz would voice 50 years later. "(In an institution) we have at best a make-believe society," said Howe, "a make-believe family, and too often a make-believe virtue; while what boys need is a real family, real society, real life, even if its virtue is not patent or approved of men." Massachusetts had boarded out its needy children or placed them in free homes in preference to institutions since 1863.

Many counties in New York State by 1918 also used boarding-out as an essential tool in caring for orphaned and destitute children. Even the city's Department of Public Charities at that date had a Children's Home Bureau that placed young children with foster families at public expense.

No, boarding-out was *not* a new idea. But when the HSGS board put Mary Boretz in charge of its reorganized Boarding and Placing-Out Bureau in 1918, *foster home care* as a professional program did not exist. Everything remained to be learned about finding the right home for a child and about supervising that home. What were the limits on the kinds of children who could benefit from foster home placement? What board rate was appropriate? What services — counseling, medical, dental, or remedial — should an agency provide? Mary Boretz was to devote the remainder of her life to finding answers and to convincing the public of the superiority of properly implemented foster home care to institutional care.

The brown-haired young woman with the flashing black eyes knew about institutions: she had been a ward herself. Her father ill with tuberculosis, her mother dead or vanished, she was admitted, at age 12, to the Brooklyn Hebrew Orphan Asylum. She had so wanted to look her best! She had starched her dress. Her hair was still crisp from the curl papers in which it had spent the night. Now she sat frozen-faced, feeling the razor pass over her scalp.

She was the top scholar in her class at the public school. But oh, the shame of delivering her graduation speech in the drab uniform and short-cropped hair that screamed "Orphan!"

Mary knew about boarding homes, too. She had lived in one after leaving the BHOA. It was probably a service home where a young girl could work for her board while attending high school. But the kindness of the people in that home was to prove a *mitzvah* to later generations of dependent children. It left their young boarder with a lifelong conviction that a foster home *could* be the best thing for a child in need of placement.

Her early belief in foster family care had been strengthened by her experiences as a cottage mother at Pleasantville. Vast improvement though it was over the orphanage of her childhood, the cottage-plan school still remained an institution. And to Mary Boretz, group living, even under the best conditions, meant a day-long subjection of personality. In the cottage, a boy never saw himself as "David" but always as a member of "the bunch." A cottage mother would not dare relieve Annie of dishwashing, irksome though that task might be to the child and willing though she might be to do other jobs. To excuse Annie might expose her cottage mother to the suspicion of playing favorites.

But in a foster home, special adjustments were easily made. Benjie, who hated oatmeal, could have something else and could begin to see himself as an individual, entitled to his own feelings. In a home, he could enjoy the affectionate attention of parents and experience the give-and-take of family relationships so necessary to his emotional development.

Mary Boretz had observed the difficulties faced by many of the Pleasantville children in their later readjustment to the community. But a child in a foster home never left the real life on the block and never had to face these painful readjustments.

The first thing Mary Boretz did, on coming to the Boarding and Placing-Out Bureau of the HSGS was to rename it. She did not want anyone to think of a foster home as temporary and the institution as the *real* home. She had the HSGS board's promise: no child happily placed in a home would be transferred to the institution. Her job was to see that the child was "happily placed." As a start, she renamed the bureau the "Home Bureau."

Skeptics were dubious. However could she find enough Jewish foster homes? Jewish families were so close-knit. They would never take a strange child on a long-term basis. And how could enough different kinds of Jewish homes be found to fit all the different kinds of children needing care?

But Mary Boretz was not worried. The second thing she did was to go to see the foster mothers she already had. There were 141 of them, with 300 children among them. Right away she discovered their attitudes left much to be desired.

Not only was it impossible for a foster mother to feel truly involved with a child who might be removed from her home at any moment; Mary Boretz discovered, too, that they were ashamed of boarding a child and hid the fact from their neighbors. "They think it's my niece or nephew visiting me. If they knew they might think my husband can't support me."

The Home Bureau would need another kind of foster mother than this! The *new* kind must be proud of her work and able to accept the idea of the central importance of her role. Mary Boretz set out to change the attitude of 141 women.

Not every foster mother could change, of course. Mary Boretz had to struggle against their shame. She insisted they had every reason to be proud. She said things like: "Without your home all our theories are useless." "You are as justified in being paid for your work as we for ours. But your contribution is *beyond payment* — a service to the whole community." She pressed the HSGS into raising the boarding rate from the two dollars a week at which it had been pegged for 14 years to $20 a month.

Only 50 of the original mothers proved able to accept the new point of view. Having spoken to each of them many times individually, Mary Boretz, in 1919, called her first foster mother's meeting.

It was an unheard of thing. To expect one foster mother to look into another's face and actually *talk* about taking care of a foster child. To think of bringing this hidden shame out into the open.

Mary Boretz had chosen her theme for that first meeting with great care. Not "What can you do for the child?" but "What has your foster child done for *you?*" She hoped that would loosen their tongues. And she was right.

Women who had never been articulate before rose to their feet to share what they had never before dared even whisper. "My Bertha, she is no angel, but she has made me twenty years younger." "I would not take a million for my Sammy. Why didn't I take him 15 years ago!"

Meetings like this became a regular part of the Home Bureau program. And soon the women themselves were helping find more homes. Shy little housewives were turning into crusaders, button-holing their friends, addressing their lodge sisters on the satisfactions of being a foster mother, looking for the "particular home" to fit the "particular child."

In March, 1922, to help foster mothers in their search for more homes, the Home Bureau published the first issue of a purse-size newsletter called the *Homefinder,* with Lucille Lazar as editor. By then Mary Boretz already had 151 foster mothers caring for 257 children. Sisters and brothers were no longer separated now but were placed in the same family whenever possible. And the women themselves were forming a Foster Mother's League to find more homes and to share experiences.

Of course, there were many ways in which foster mothers had to be educated. The importance of proper medical and dental care was not always clear to them — even though the Home Bureau provided the doctor and the dentist. How foolish to take a girl who had no toothache to a dentist!

Simple patience and tolerance also had to be encouraged. It might be a while before a child was ready to give affection. The foster mother must be willing to wait. And habits of cleanliness did not come overnight to a boy raised by a chronically ailing mother in a home without a bath.

For many an older woman, it was difficult to accept help and advice from the much younger "visitor." Over and over the case-worker had to explain that the knowledge shared was not simply her own notion but had been accumulated by older and wiser minds.

Many practices needed to be worked out for the newly developing discipline. How frequently should the worker visit? Soon older children were being seen twice a month; at that age a quarrel between child and foster parent might precipitate a gulf difficult to heal without prompt help. For younger children, one visit a month could be enough — fewer for one child if another needed it more. Schools, clinics and social service agencies had to be visited, too.

How do you teach true respect for children? By example, of course. The Home Bureau had to show that *it* valued the children it placed in homes. No longer was clothing purchased in job lots. Instead a member of the Home Bureau committee went shopping from manufacturer to manufacturer picking out every dress, every suit, so each child could look like an individual. And that clothing belonged to *that* child to care for and outgrow. Birthday parties, too, must be celebrated. Many a child was given its first party in a foster home. The children of the Home Bureau are not "poor orphans," said Mary Boretz. Children have no obligation to be grateful. They deserve all the good things they get.

The real parent also had to be considered. Gone was the day when a child was dumped on the doorstep of the HSGS by the

Department of Public Welfare and shipped to a boarding home without any discussion with the family. Real parents were important. Mary Boretz always saw any that could be found before placing the child and urged the parent — it was usually a father — to visit his child regularly.

Frequently the parent was hostile. Many preferred institutions. At least the child would have good medical care and education and be taught proper manners in an institution. A foster home was an unknown factor. Moreover it meant a competing set of parents and perhaps a need for the real parent to feel obligated. In any case, the woman was only doing it for money! "She'll let my children run wild in the streets," was the complaint Mary Boretz heard, over and over.

Sunday morning of each week (the Sabbath having been duly celebrated on Saturday) was reserved at the Home Bureau as "parents' complaint morning." The parent was asked to visit his child in the foster home but not to tell the foster mother if he had complaints; instead he was to "Come back and let it out on us."

At first there was continuous fault-finding, but gradually cooperation and understanding took its place. Mary Boretz always recalled the father who entered furious at hearing that his little son had been transferred from the infants' institution. The boy must immediately be returned to him! He would not permit him to stay in a foster home in the city.

Mary Boretz knew about this man. She knew he had seen one son killed and another hurt on the streets. He had good reason to be afraid. She didn't argue with him. Instead she gave him a letter of discharge to the foster mother and told him to go visit the child. If he was not satisfied, he could give the foster mother the letter and take his boy.

Two days later, Mary Boretz received the letter of discharge in the mail with a grateful note from the father. He had found his boy living in a safe suburban home where there was no reason to fear his being killed or injured.

In those first few years, Mary Boretz fought many battles within the HSGS. Those who worked with her in the early days remember the impatience with which she attacked the old entrenched ways.

She never waited for things to change; she changed them. "She flashed. You couldn't miss the lightning," recalls her long-time secretary, Helen Sigman.

Some of her earliest battles were with the doctor at the city office of the HSGS, who examined all the children brought there. It was his job to decide whether a child was "okay" for placement either at Pleasantville or in a home. Since the Home Bureau shared the city office of the institution, this doctor and Mary Boretz saw a lot of each other.

One day, the young woman escorted a newly admitted little girl to the barber. But instead of allowing him to shave the child's head, she had him give her an attractive medium-long bob. The doctor was outraged. But he had to admit shaving heads was an obsolete practice. It was just that no one had ever bothered to challenge it before. From that day on, the HSGS children were permitted hair like other children.

Another battle of Mary Boretz' concerned the children with serious physical defects. She saw them brought in by the Department of Welfare to be examined for admission by the doctor. And she saw him reject them. The HSGS had never accepted cardiac cases, children suffering from the nervous disease called chorea (St. Vitus Dance), or severely handicapped children.

Lucille Lazar recalls one particular little girl with a cardiac condition who was brought back, time and again. The child shuttled back and forth between the city hospital on Blackwell's Island and the HSGS office — only to be repeatedly turned down. She remembers also two boys — the one crippled by polio hobbled in on crutches; the other was diabetic. The doctor rejected both.

"Your job," Mary Boretz informed him, "is to tell me what they need. My job is to find it."

That year, the Home Bureau found a home for the cardiac girl. In later years, it sometimes had as many as 400 chronically ill children in care at one time. They suffered from all kinds of ailments — arrested forms of childhood tuberculosis, asthma, skin diseases, polio and other crippling ailments, ear infections, endocrine conditions, hypertension, and, of course, cardiac conditions.

Mary Boretz believed that a good and understanding home could be found for almost *any* child — and almost always she was right.

Mary Boretz battled for her foster parents, too, exerting constant pressure on the Board to raise the boarding rate. She pushed it up to $22 a month, then $25. For a while, Federation made up the difference between the HSGS rate and what the Department of Public Welfare was willing to pay. But at last the city raised its rate — and foster parents of all faiths could benefit from Mary Boretz' determined championship of foster home care.

Soon Pleasantville also was sending the Home Bureau those of its children under 16 who were ready to attend the city high schools. (The public school that had replaced Dr. Bernstein's original program only went through eighth grade.) For the girls, Mary Boretz adapted Friendship House's idea of "opportunity homes." But the Home Bureau gave the foster mother money to pay the girl for her work, knowing that earned money helped build the adolescent's self-confidence.

A legendary Home Bureau figure for 24 years was Mamie Goldfarb who left her job as a cottage mother at Pleasantville in 1919 to head the bureau's clothing department. Twice a year the children came in to get their medical exam and to select, with her help, all-new outfits from the assortment of styles and colors she and a volunteer had chosen. (A child extra hard on clothes might get a *few* second hand articles in addition.)

Large, warm, and authoritarian, the wardrobe mistress was never too busy to listen to a foster parent's problems — and advise and scold. Although she had not learned Yiddish as a child, in her new role she soon spoke it so fluently that foster mothers frequently asked what part of Russia she came from — and believed her when she claimed to come from their own home town. What a day it was when Mrs. Goldfarb set out on her yearly trip to the circus with 100 children in tow! And there was always room in her apartment above the Home Bureau office for a child or two waiting for a foster home.

By 1922, when the Clearing Bureau opened, the Home Bureau had grown considerably. Mary Boretz now had a professional staff of five field workers, one trained nurse, a resident worker, a part-time physician (her husband Dr. Henry Friedman) — and an office staff. Formerly half the children from the boarding homes had been sent on to Pleasantville. But of the 405 children cared for by the Home Bureau since 1918, only 13 had been transferred to the cottage school. Eleven of these had gone to Pleasantville to be with brothers and sisters; only two because they had proved too hard to handle in a home. Best of all, in her report to the HSGS Board that year, Mary Boretz could say: "We reject no child except for contagious disease or definite mental defect."

That year Herman Block clearly restated the position of the HSGS Board: "(The Bureau) has been instructed to place as many children as possible in foster homes, providing such homes are of the high standards we demand and are adequately supervised by trained professional workers. The (Home Bureau) Committee has been instructed to carry on the work without regard to the number of vacancies that may exist in Pleasantville and to keep in mind one aim only — the best interest of the child."

But the battle to translate this attitude to the other large Manhattan institutions—to the HOA and the Home for Hebrew Infants — began with the coming of the Clearing Bureau. The Hebrew Orphan Asylum, with its enormous, beautifully tended building, was still preoccupied with the problem of empty beds. It had a foster home bureau, but it continued to call it the "Boarding-Out Bureau" and to subordinate it to the needs of the institution.

Alice Seligsberg, the director of the Clearing Bureau, of course knew this. She sent many children to the Home Bureau. But she was reluctant to "recommend" children to the HOA's Boarding-Out Bureau. All HOA children were admitted through the institution's reception house. It was difficult for her to be certain where they went from there. She suspected most of them ended up filling an empty bed in the institution — no matter what her recommendation.

Time and again Superintendent Lionel Simmonds promised to let her know exactly what happened to each child. But his reports failed to materialize. As late as 1928, the president of the asylum in his annual report was still hewing to the idea that "children boarded out, except in the homes of the finer type, do not receive the many benefits that the children are receiving in our institution, especially in character building from the angle of religious training, general instruction, health, habit formation and regularity of life."

But that proved to be a losing argument. When Sally Melnick went to work at the HOA Boarding-Out Bureau in 1925, she found 6 or 8 workers. By 1940 there were 32 (including clerical help) and many empty beds in the institution.

She remembers sharp struggles along the way. Over spring coats for boarding home children, for instance. It was difficult for an orphanage superintendent to see why HOA wards would need spring coats. But the trustees saw her point. The children had to look like other children in their community. They received spring coats.

Across the river and safe from the insistent pressures of the Clearing Bureau — since Brooklyn institutions were not members — the Brooklyn Hebrew Orphan Asylum also slowly moved toward accepting the importance of foster home care. It had had a temporary boarding bureau for children under six since 1912. At six the healthy ones were transferred to the institution. In 1927 this changed. The BHOA hired its first professional social worker, Evelyn Ferdeber, to head a reorganized "Child Placement Bureau" and started placing children of all ages in foster homes.

It was the trend of the times. Even the American Legion at its 1923 convention had come out for family care. "An institution is bad for children," read the Legion's statement, "because the single child is not important there. It is always nice to plan big things, but children want small things that belong to them and to which they belong."

In 1915, with a New York City population of about 5,200,000, there had been 20,417 city children in the care of children's institutions and agencies, with public subsidy. By 1925, the population had soared a million — to 6,200,000. Yet, thanks to Widows Pensions and foster homes (and in part no doubt to the sharp drop in immigration), the number of children in care had dropped to 12,500.

There were other pressures forcing change on institutions for Jewish children, after the First World War. For one thing the children committed no longer had the same problems as before. For another, the growing disciplines of developmental psychology and psychiatry were insisting on a more careful evaluation of the individual child and the crucial importance of meeting the child's emotional needs in the early years. The agencies were being asked to tool up for more specialized care.

# Chapter 6

# What Kind of Institution?

*". . . it would have been tragic . . . if in the enthusiasm for the foster family which swept the country in the 1930's all institutions had been swept away."* ALAN KEITH-LUCAS, THE ANNALS OF THE AMERICAN ACADEMY OF POLITICAL AND SOCIAL SCIENCE, SEPTEMBER, 1964.

NINE-YEAR OLD SIMON GIRTLER, born in Russia, and his five-year old New York-born brother, Solomon, were typical of children admitted to the city's Jewish institutions in the thirty years before the First World War. Their widowed mother, Betsy, age 37, was forced to work long hours as a seamstress and so, according to the entry of October 27, 1897 in the HOA admissions book, was "not able to bring up her youngest children."

By the early twenties, this immigrant situation was no longer typical. The war had sharply cut the flow of newcomers. After the war restrictive immigration laws prevented any resumption of the mass flight from Eastern Europe to the United States. The first temporary restrictive act was passed in 1921. The national-origins-quota act followed in 1924. It would remain in force for 40 years. Supporters of such laws were frank as to their reasons. Persons of non-Nordic stock were seen as inferior and less assimilable than other national stocks, while immigrants from Bolshevik Russia were viewed also as potential revolutionary plotters.

As a result, the Jewish youngster needing care more likely now came from a family resident in the United States for some years. And, as we have seen, destitution was no longer reason enough for the commitment of any Jewish child. Widows' Pensions and funds from the United Hebrew Charities and the Widowed Mothers' Funds Association (which helped non-citizens) enabled the Betsy Girtlers at least to keep their families together.

Moreover, thanks to the Clearing Bureau and the new policy of the HSGS, the kind of children most desired by the institutions were now more often "recommended" to foster homes. So that those entering the HOA, and most especially the Pleasantville institution, were frequently the youngsters with marked psychological problems, coming from families with lengthening histories of marital and social maladjustment.

Like those who had gone before, such children were a product of *their* times. The social upheavals of the war, the depression and unemployment that introduced and followed it, the Red witch hunts that agitated American society in the wake of the Bolshevik Revolution, and the climate of fear and uncertainty all these created — served to weaken homes that were too often themselves the fragile offspring of earlier immigrant hardship. But, fortunately for the children, the ideas pioneered by Sigmund Freud now were modifying the way in which society viewed those who failed comfortably to conform.

The Second White House Conference on Children, in 1919, had called for pioneering action in the field of child guidance and juvenile courts. Three years later, New York State responded with the "Children's Court Act" establishing courts for children separate and distinct from the criminal courts. Psychiatrists and psychologists were attached to these new courts which were to serve not only delinquent but also neglected and mentally defective children.

Psychologists and psychiatrists were being appointed to Jewish institutions and foster home services, too. In 1920, Pleasantville added a member of each of these professions on a part-time basis. In 1923, the Home Bureau opened a "Mental Hygiene Clinic" with a part-time psychologist. The HOA had opened a psychological clinic earlier, in 1916, and had begun also to offer vocational and educational guidance services. By 1925, it, too, had a "Mental Hygiene Clinic" under the direction of a "psycho-pediatrician." The BHOA followed suit a few years later.

These new departments were purely diagnostic, mainly intended to eliminate severely disturbed and retarded children. No treatment was provided. In fact, very little was known about techniques for treating troubled children. It was a little-explored field. But the need for trained diagnostic skills was recognized.

The need for casework training was gaining equal recognition, and had been greatly spurred by the First World War. Where, in 1915, there were only five independent social work training schools and two attached to universities, by 1919 there were 29 schools throughout the country. Two years later, social workers organized the American Association of Social Workers. The association immediately turned to studying, defining and standardizing positions in social work. Trained workers were growing in number. Professional knowledge was increasing. But there was still a long way to go.

There were several reasons why the change in the type of children committed to Jewish institutions should first have been noticed at Pleasantville. The Clearing Bureau preferred to entrust the more "nervous" and difficult children to the more intimate cottage atmosphere rather than to the huge HOA. And the HSGS board itself now followed a policy of placing the "normal" child under 10 in a foster home. But it was also true that in a cottage institution the child with problems stood out more clearly and atypical behavior was more likely to cause concern.

As a result, so many disturbed children had surfaced at Pleasantville by 1925 that the director, Dr. Leon Goldrich, asked the board to appoint a psychiatric panel to discuss steps for dealing with the problem.

The idea of isolating disturbed children from the more "normal" ones struck everyone as unpleasant. But how were the former affecting the overall program? It was essential to know. How should the school go about finding the answer?

The panel appointed was headed by Freud's disciple, Dr. A. A. Brill. It recommended working quietly, allowing professionals to study the children but without drawing any special attention either to the problem or to the children. Dr. Clarence P. Oberndorff, Chief of Psychiatry at Mount Sinai, agreed to direct the psychiatric study and a young psychologist and psychiatric social worker named Julia Goldman moved to Pleasantville to set up a "Mental Hygiene and Child Guidance Department" under his guidance.

Dr. Oberndorff assured Miss Goldman she could return to her job as head of Mount Sinai's mental health clinic within a year. In fact, she was to remain at Pleasantville 16 years.

A shy but tenacious person, Julia Goldman recalls the first six weeks of her new assignment as "hellish." Despite Dr. Goldrich's wholehearted backing, her presence was greeted by almost everyone else with hostility and suspicion.

Who ever heard of a mental health clinic in a children's institution? Hadn't they been doing all right before?

Buttressed by Dr. Goldrich and by the sympathy and practical guidance of Dr. Oberndorff, the clinic's young executive worked slowly, always careful not to force herself on anyone. Both children and staff had to be permitted to discover at their own pace that she was not dangerous, merely available if they needed help.

She was a quiet figure, living in a children's cottage, walking around campus, visiting classrooms, eating in the staff dining room, and, evenings, dropping in at various cottages.

First to abandon their suspicions were the children. Then, one by one, the teachers asked her help with problems in class — "They had so many!" she recalls. Last of all, the cottage mothers opened up.

Now the work could really start. Because only the cottage mothers and the teachers really knew which children needed help.

By the end of that first year, the clinic had, in addition to Julia Goldman, one psychologist, three psychiatrists, and two social workers. All except the psychiatrists lived at the institution. It was the first psychiatric clinic established in any American child care institution, and, according to Miss Goldman, the only one anywhere, at that time, available both day and night.

As the children came under closer scrutiny, the caseload grew. Closer examination of a child who made no overt trouble often unmasked deep-seated problems. At first, the clinic staff estimated about 50 out of the approximately 300 children were in need of treatment. At the end of two years, the caseload, including children being seen on a consultation basis or kept under supervision, was 170, with a monthly active load of 60. By the end of 1929, over 28% of the 280 children at Pleasantville were in treatment.

The question now was: Had the institution reached its saturation point for this kind of child? How many could Pleasantville well accept without losing the "normal" environment which was so essential a part of the therapeutic plan?

The original estimate had been that 15% disturbed children was the maximum that could be absorbed. But the very existence and reputation of the clinic attracted more and more requests for admission. "The courts pleaded; the schools pleaded," says Julia Goldman. "Take just one more child!"

A major undertaking was the training of cottage mothers to help in treatment. Lectures and discussions conveyed some theoretical knowledge. Later, the very qualifications for the position of cottage parent were redefined. The cottage was assigned a key role in the treatment plan, and the entire institution was involved.

The clinic also influenced changes in the sports program, always rather neglected in the past. Now football, soccer and, for girls, volleyball became important therapeutic activities.

The transformed institution soon was receiving new plaudits. In 1927, the inspector of the State Board of Charities praised its pioneering spirit. Two years later, gratified with the experiment's progress, the inspector expressed his hope that other institutions would "unconditionally imitate" Pleasantville's example. In 1938, both Judge Rosalie L. Whitney of the City's Domestic Relations Court and Dr. Lauretta Bender, Director of the Children's Ward of Bellevue Hospital's Psychiatric Division, applauded the institution's program, describing it as "almost indispensable" as a resource for children. By this time, Dr. Bender was referring psychiatric cases to Pleasantville from her children's ward.

It was primarily the professional community who were aware of these changes in Pleasantville's program and population. To the general public, the school continued to be known as an outstanding institution for orphaned or dependent children. Even with the majority of its children under treatment, the therapeutic program was never obvious.

By 1930, Dr. Goldrich, originally a high school principal, had become one of the nation's leading experts on child guidance. At the invitation of New York City's Board of Education, he left Pleasantville to set up a new Bureau of Child Guidance for the City's school system.

When Julia Goldman replaced him as Pleasantville's director, she set about further liberalizing the lives of the children. Dr. Goldrich already had considerably reduced the emphasis on scholastic achievement which had been such an important part of Dr. Bernstein's philosophy. But the new director now questioned why the boys' cottages all should be on one side of the square, the girls on the other. And why shouldn't boys and girls be allowed to roam the spacious acres together? Those heavy blue serge bloomers that turned even the most graceful girl into an elephant — were they really necessary? And the reception house — why two or three *weeks* of isolation for a new child when public health experts now felt two or three days was plenty? And why not a weekly bus to take the children into town for home visits, instead of the irregular planning of the past?

For the youngest wards, a "toyery" was installed where a child could borrow a toy as he or she might a book from the library. The borrower's record card included information on the toy's condition. Any broken toy had to be repaired by the children themselves in the vocational classes.

And now, in the middle of the depression, Pleasantville got a band! A vigorous search by a former alumnus, William Singer, unearthed a box of assorted musical instruments with dates ranging back to the year 1885. Eager hands polished and mended and cleaned and scraped. Cracked instruments were carefully soldered. Within the year, 30 budding musicians were parading around campus proudly blaring their single song. The next year, Armonk's American Legion Post feverishly sought their talents at the last moment to replace a fife and drum corps lost to a higher bidder. With that as a spur, the band turned professional. After six days of furious practice, they paraded, earned $25 and local fame. Within three years the new music program had involved over 300 children.

Another innovation was the employment of young men as assistants to the cottage mothers in each boys' cottage. In the forties, cottage fathers were introduced for the boys.

While Pleasantville was liberalizing its program and developing into a noted psychiatric treatment center, the HOA, too, was further relaxing the stern regimentation which originally had been thought a necessity in any large institution. To the extent that it could, it, too, was individualizing its handling of its children.

The liberalizing process had started back in 1905 with Superintendent Solomon Loewenstein and had accelerated under his successor, former ward Lionel Simmonds. The "rising bell" that incessantly commanded children to stand or sit, the harsh punishments for bed-wetting, the crowded 100-bed dormitories, the military line-ups, the endless dining tables with their endless benches — all were gone by the mid-twenties.

Huge dormitories were broken up into alcoves of 20 beds. Small tables and chairs were introduced for dining. And the ratio of staff to children was vastly improved. In 1910, there was one counselor to 100 children. By 1921, there were two counselors and two junior counselors (usually part-time college students) for the same number of children. Hair was no longer close-cropped; clothing was more varied and better fitting. Even visiting days were changed! "Every day is visiting day," announced the HOA president in his 1928 report, "Provided the parents are respectable, they can see their children at any time when not at school." The importance of maintaining family contact in order to hasten later readjustment was at last being recognized.

In 1909, the HOA, with the help of its Junior League, had opened a rest home at Ardsley for fattening up its underweight and anemic children. In 1910, it opened another at Woodlands (later moved to Valhalla). These were discontinued in 1919, when it established two summer camps on the Bear Mountain Interstate Reservation — ten years before the state legislature introduced a bill advocating such camps for "children of the deserving poor." With the help of the Indian Department at the American Museum of Natural History, Wakitan — "perseverance" — was picked as a properly inspiring name for the boys' camp. But the name of the girls' camp had to begin with a "W", too, in order that honor pins and insignia could be bought in bulk. So Wehaha — "laughing waters" — was selected by the camp's first director, HOA alumnus Lester Loeb.

Generous endowments and rich friends made many enhancements possible. One of the Warner brothers donated a fine gymnasium with movie projection facilities. Visits to Broadway, to ballgames and the circus became weekly occurrences. The Godmothers' Association, formed in 1921, started clubs for the teen-age girls which met weekly in the homes of the volunteers. And, by 1922, almost any ward interested could be assured of a continuing vocational or academic education financed by a scholarship grant, if she or he showed aptitude. By that time, the HOA had 51 especially endowed trusts — most of them for educational purposes and two boasting $100,000 endowments.

There was concern with aftercare, too, at the HOA by the twenties, although this concern was far less casework-oriented than at Fellowship House. The first aftercare worker had been hired in 1915. By 1920, the worker was expected to follow-up for at least three years any young person discharged.

In 1916, the Ladies Sewing Society — their former function made obsolete by technological advance — had opened a Friendly Home for Girls to teach older HOA girls household skills. After six months live-in training, the young women were placed in service homes while they completed high school or vocational training.

In 1917 the HOA's Junior League had opened the Cornerhouse for Boys (later the Lavanburg Corner House) on Charles Street in Greenwich Village.

By 1922, there were dances, too, where the boys could meet the girls. And even better — because strictly illegal — was the secret rendezvous in the Captain's Den in the HOA basement, with a boy posted outside to watch for prying staff.

The BHOA, with far less endowment than the HOA, was undergoing similar liberalization in children's appearance and general living environment. The women's auxiliary could report in 1922 that all but 27 of the girls now had dancing slippers and "provision will be made for same." As a former ward of the HOA, the young superintendent, Aaron Jacoby, also was quick to reform the visiting rules — although the board had first to be convinced. Now mothers no longer had to smuggle food in; they could carry it openly. And parents could visit whenever they pleased. "They never abused the privilege," recalls the former superintendent. There was a summer home at Rockaway Park, an indoor gymnasium and a magazine, the *Pathfinder,* published by the children themselves. For the girls discharged with no homes to return to, a small group of women — most of them wives of BHOA trustees — had, by 1915, founded the Girls Club.

Although profoundly patriarchal in their approach, the HOA and the BHOA nevertheless were growing increasingly sophisticated in their understanding of their wards' needs. And for particular children, especially at the wealthy HOA — for the frailest and the ablest —there could be considerable personal attention. In fact, such children had received special care for at least a decade before the twenties. One HOA alumnus — let's call him Saul — remembers very well the help he received when he was brought to the HOA in 1911, suffering from rickets and anemia and, at 7½, almost mute.

He previously had spent four years at the New York Child's Nursery and Hospital, and, to this day, recalls no earlier life — except for a shadowy scene around a table with everyone hovering solicitously over his cut finger. Many little "Sauls" were admitted to the HOA, and had a variety of experiences, some good, some not so good.

Not long after he arrived, the HOA placed him for several weeks at its country home and farm in Ardsley, before sending him for five months to the HOA rest home at Valhalla.

When he was placed in school, his speech problem held him in the same grade for two years. No one nagged or pushed. Gradually, as he grew accustomed to the other children and the speech buzzing so eagerly around him, he started to talk himself and made good progress in school.

The HOA became his only family. He had never known his father and had not seen his mother for years. Still, for a while, he continued to hope when visiting time came around that his would be among the names called. It never was — until one day, he took a shower at an unscheduled time. When he emerged, he learned that his mother had been there to see him. She never came again.

In time he became a monitor, then a captain of monitors — and, as was the custom, used all the army type methods to compel conformity. But something happened to Saul. He had been one of those chosen to attend the Speyer Junior High School, the first experimental junior high for intellectually gifted children run by the Board of Education. Was it learning Latin as a spoken language, listening to Beethoven in music appreciation, or idolizing his English teacher? At any rate, *something* changed, and Saul began to rebel at the regimentation of HOA life.

At 18, chafing at living in the institution, Saul was obligingly placed by the over-paternalistic HOA in a boarding home. When he found himself unhappy in the home, the administration transferred him to the Lavanburg Corner House.

By now Saul was a student at City College and loathing every moment of it, especially the ROTC, omnipresent and compulsory in those days. Still anxious to be helpful, Papa HOA dipped into the family coffers and this time offered its restive charge a scholarship to any East Coast college that would take him.

But by this time the young man preferred to try his own wings. He headed West, working his way through Stanford University, and Reed College. Back in New York he earned an M.A. in English at Columbia and an M.S.S. from the Graduate School of Jewish Social Work. He went on to a distinguished career in the field of Jewish social work.

But Saul — at first because of his health problem, later because of his liveliness and intelligence — was an attention-getting child. The mass of children — those who could get by well enough and demanded no special attention — they were the ones whose individuality suffered most from the routinized, often impersonal institutional life, even in a liberalized HOA.

Nevertheless, by the mid-twenties, there was one kind of child that the HOA knew had to have special attention. That was the retarded child. Every congregate institution had a few — shoved out of the way, half ignored.

Unable to keep up in school retarded children led a miserable life. Scorned in the institution by children their own age for being immature, rejected by younger ones for being too old they received no individual help. Some did better in foster homes. But when the time came for these to move out on their own, the aftercare workers found it impossible to help. Having received no special training or education, few could find a job. When they did, they could not hold it. Because they were such an easy target for men, retarded girls were especially worrisome. The HOA decided to start by helping these.

In 1918, the institution had purchased 123 acres of land and an old colonial house in the Edenwald section of the Bronx, with the intention of moving all its wards to a cottage institution for 1200 children to be built there at a cost of $4,000,000. But Federation had frowned on the idea of a separate public appeal for funds by one of its member agencies. Instead a United Building Fund campaign was organized, which netted the HOA only $1,000,000 as its share. The difficulty of soliciting further contributions from friends in the middle of the post-war depression had discouraged even the most eager HOA board members. But the dream of an enormous cottage institution persisted until 1922 when the Bureau of Jewish Social Research released a child care study undertaken for Federation's Child Care Committee.

The study — which included the HOA, HSGS, and HHI — emphasized the importance of keeping children out of institutions and strongly urged finding more ways to keep families together. It recommended a merging of the HSGS and HOA foster home systems and stated that institutional care was needed for only about 900 Jewish children in Manhattan.

Neither HOA nor HSGS was prepared to merge foster home units — yet. But the HOA board abandoned its plan for a new plant and, instead, began to expand its boarding-out department.

It was then, also — and now with the full support of Federation — that the board decided to remodel the old colonial house at Edenwald and there establish a special facility for retarded girls. A house mother and vocational teacher were selected, a teacher for the academic courses obtained through the Board of Education, and a married couple employed. The woman was to teach cooking and laundry work, her husband to work as handyman and teach farming.

In May, 1925, the Edenwald School for Girls opened with fifteen girls between 15 and 16 years of age, chosen from among the retarded HOA wards. By the end of the year, the HOA knew it had made a mistake. If training was to be useful to a youngster of this kind, it had to be started earlier in life.

The next year, a second group of 15 girls were moved to the Bronx property. This time no girl was older than 12. The program went so well that within a few months, 13 more girls were added.

The basic philosophy was simple: the retarded girl must be taught to take care of herself and to make her way in the community. Endless patience, ready praise, and visible results would be the ingredients that made for progress.

Useful practical skills — laundry, cooking, housework, simple farming — were stressed and learned through daily practice. Work in a more advanced field for which a girl also had received training might not always be available.

In groups of three, the girls marketed, shopped with the teacher for sewing materials, attended movies or the theatre, travelled to the HOA for dental or medical treatment. Parents were encouraged to visit and take the child home overnight.

As she showed aptitude, each girl was helped to learn more complicated skills. From simple sewing, by hand and machine, she might advance into dressmaking or millinery work. Rugs were woven and an entire room decorated with materials tie-dyed by the girls themselves. Everything a girl made was for her personal use or for the house she lived in.

Late in 1928, four young women were graduated and placed with firms manufacturing women's clothing. A few months later, the aftercare worker proudly reported they were still employed.

But not all the children did so well. Some seemed not to be helped at all. There were no special techniques — other than patient repetition — for overcoming learning blocks.

Still a beginning had been made. The next April, the HOA, greatly encouraged, added a separate school for boys on the same property.

It was 1929. The stock market crashed in October. The worst depression in history had started. Before long, children would see grown men and women standing in line on street corners — waiting for bread, waiting for jobs. Unemployed fathers slumped dejectedly at home. Families evicted from their homes for non-payment of rent built shacks of tin and lumber scraps on the banks of the Hudson and the East rivers. Rootless young men swarmed the roads, looking for work. Nowhere were there jobs or a future for young people.

# The Battling
# Thirties

*"To merge or not to merge—that in New York Jewish child-care circles has been the boiling, broiling, sizzling question for the short period of only 20 years. . . . (Our) efforts have resulted in a 100% BATTLING average—not a single merger has been effected."*
HERMAN W. BLOCK, ADDRESSING NATIONAL COUNCIL OF FEDERATIONS FOR THE SUPPORT OF JEWISH PHILANTHROPIC SOCIETIES, PHILADELPHIA, JANUARY 28, 1937.

T HE PERIOD so painfully remembered as "The Great Depression" brought critical new problems to those concerned with New York City's dependent Jewish children and accentuated old problems. But the struggle it forced on the child-care professionals in the end brought great benefits, too. Public measures benefitting children — measures that had been only dreams in 1929 — by the end of the decade were won and already taken for granted.

The struggle furnished a crucible for skills and existing programs; it refined old ones, demanded new ones, and glaringly exposed those that were obsolete. In doing so, it further spurred the development of the social work profession. And in 1940, the first giant step at last was taken toward a merger of the New York Jewish community's services to its dependent children, a merger sought by some since 1917.

But few could have guessed, during the terrible three years that followed the crash, that social advances would spring from the accelerating disaster.

As the institutions and the foster home staffs saw their 16-year old graduates spinning off into a society that mercilessly buffeted even the stable and experienced adult, the major burden of attempting to cope with chaos fell on the aftercare workers.

The great strength of Fellowship House had always been its ability to find work for the children discharged from Pleasantville and the Home Bureau. Suddenly, there *was* no work. Even youngsters already employed were being dismissed or forced to work under worse conditions for less pay. And what sparse public and private relief programs existed were overwhelmed by the landslide of need. Nor, at first, were there even social and recreational programs to serve the thousands of idle young. The task of helping young people was threatened by a world that defeated every attempt to achieve independence.

More aftercare boarding homes were urgently needed, too, because more of the children's own homes were proving unliveable. Parents, driven frantic by their own joblessness, often refused to understand why a youngster could not find work.

For a girl, there was still the "service" boarding home. But the homes themselves had to be more carefully supervised. They tended to be more exploitative than in the past. Domestic workers, after all, were a drug on the market. Many experienced workers had no choice but to labor for little more than their food.

In the absence of any substantial government help, Fellowship House and the aftercare departments of the other Jewish agencies made yeoman efforts to salvage their youth. Scholarships and loans for further education and training not only offered long-range career possibilities. Although schools were swamped with adolescents over 16 and classes badly overcrowded, they spared young people the daily anguish of looking for work that did not exist. For a few, "made work" could be obtained from agency supporters and friends, but never enough to make a dent. Workshops, too, were set up to keep some off the streets. And occasionally cash relief was provided by Fellowship House, often with the help of the volunteer women who called themselves the Guardian Mothers.

A child in crisis, and with no place to go, might end up in Sarah Sussman's home until other plans could be made. It was beyond the call of duty, but the executive secretary of Fellowship House was a social worker of the old school who still recalls, as a young woman, making barley soup and washing clothes for harassed clients — despite her supervisor's insistence that such behavior was "unprofessional." In 1961, on receiving Federation's Israel Cummings Award as the outstanding Jewish social worker of the year, she summed up her philosophy in one sentence: "I believe with perfect faith that I *am* my brother's keeper."

Understandably, more children than ever required intensive counseling during those difficult years. But practical guidance was the best even Fellowship House — with its four caseworkers — could offer most of its charges. And there were few "practical" answers.

In 1932, the aftercare agency somewhat desperately started its own work relief project for boys, on an abandoned farm. Later this was moved to the estate of Louis Kahn in South Salem. With food from the state's new Temporary Emergency Relief Administration; a few workers provided by the equally new Emergency Work Bureau; and some assistance from Pleasantville's new alumni association, the Crows and Ravens, it set up the Sylvan Stix Workshop, named after the Fellowship House president. In effect, the camp proved to be a miniature model for the later federal Civilian Conservation Corps. Young men from other agencies also were enrolled, including, in 1934, three black youths—the first in the Jewish agency's history.

The young campers converted a barn into a mess hall, built a kitchen, installed plumbing, flooded a meadow for a swimming area, cleared land for a ball field and developed an ambitious agricultural program. The workshop proved so valuable that it was continued as a summer project through 1949.

When President Roosevelt took office in 1933 and federal relief programs began to be introduced on a massive scale, the task of the aftercare workers was considerably eased. But home relief — a meager stipend — still often had to be supplemented with money for a young person's carfare and other incidental needs. And, sometimes, the agency still would provide the relief itself, in order to spare a particularly fragile young person humiliations that might undo all the gains made at Pleasantville or in a foster home.

Nevertheless the new programs developed by the federal Works Project Administration, the Civilian Conservation Corps, and the National Youth Administration increasingly made it possible to direct young people into valid work and educational opportunities, leaving the aftercare staff free to give more of their time to children who needed more than jobs or training or economic help.

Occasionally, cooperation between agency and government brought resounding successes. In 1937, with the help of a director from the Federal Theatre Project, Fellowship House celebrated its 25th Anniversary with an original musical comedy whose cast was 50 youngsters in aftercare.

Book, songs and lyrics for the comedy, "Oh, Spinach," which was presented at a Broadway theatre, were contributed by a former caseworker, Sylvia Golden.

But the federal programs that helped stem the crisis were emergency programs. They provided no sure means toward a future. Of more lasting value were the later New Deal measures designed to buttress families against future economic disaster. The Federal Unemployment Insurance, Old Age and Survivors Insurance, and Aid to Dependent Children included in the Social Security Act passed August, 1935, made it far easier to keep families together, in bad times as well as good.

Results were not seen overnight. It took more than two years for admissions to the Home Bureau to be affected. But during 1938 the number dropped a precipitous 30% — a change at least partially attributable to implementation of the new measures.

For many families and their children, however, such protective laws came too late. The damage was done. As the depression continued, the institutions and foster homes found themselves admitting an ever growing percentage of disturbed children.

In its 1936 bi-annual report, the HSGS noted that while only 30% of those admitted to Pleasantville in 1932 were classified as "disturbed," by 1935 — after the worst was past — the figure was 68%. And the typical entering complaint now was that a child could not be managed at home. Children committed for such reasons betrayed strong feelings of rejection.

A similar phenomenon was noticed in the foster homes. From 1932 to 1934, during the bleakest years of the depression, emergency public relief seemed to be keeping larger numbers of families together. But the Home Bureau's May, 1936 report gave a very different picture. Even as the apparatus was being set up for

The first home of the Hebrew Orphan Asylum, altered over the years, still stands on 29th Street, just west of Eighth Avenue.

(above, left) Mordecai Manuel Noah, president of the Hebrew Benevolent Society, 1842-1851.

(below, left) Philip J. Joachimsen and his wife, Priscilla, founders of the Hebrew Sheltering Guardian Society, of which she was the first president.

| 1881. | | |
|---|---|---|
| Nov. 15 | Barnard, George | Inattentive |
| 22 | Brown, Louis | Very disorderly |
| 23 | Brown Abraham | Trifling |
| 30 | Brown, Louis | Bad Conduct |
| Dec 5 | Bleichman Isidore | Troublesome |
| 5 | Brown, Louis | Very disorderly |
| 12 | Brown, Louis | Disorder, impertinent |
| | Blum, Alfred | Very troublesome |
| 13 | Brown Louis | Disorder |
| 14 | Blum, Alfred | Very bad conduct |
| 19 | Barnard, Geo. | Conduct very poor all day and is very indifferent about it |
| 21 | Bergman, Louis | Very disorderly |
| 1882 | | |
| Jan. 9 | Bergman, Louis | Disorderly |
| 17 | Bergman, Louis | disorderly |
| Feb 20 | Berliner | Speaking |
| 24 | Bergman, Louis | Talking |
| 28 | Berliner, Benjamin | Disorder |
| Mch 2 | Bergman, Louis | Incessant talking |
| 3 | Berliner, Benjamin | Disorder and disobedience |
| 6 | Brown, Louis | Disorderly Conduct |
| 8 | Bergman, Louis | Deceitful |
| 13 | Brown, Abraham | Very disorderly |
| 16 | Brown, Louis | Disorder |

| 1882. | | |
|---|---|---|
| April 18 | Blum, Alfred | Very troublesome |
| 18 | Berliner, Benjamin | Stayed in school without permission |
| 20 | Berliner, Benjamin | Disorder. Th— away the pass and forget another for 2 |
| May 1 | Brown Abr. | Disorderly |
| | Bergman L. | Troublesome |
| 3 | Berliner Benj. | Disorderly |
| | Brieger Isaac | No Pass |
| 4 | Brown, Abraham | Disorder |
| 22 | Beck, Siegmund | Not Excellent |
| 22 | Brown, Abraham | Very Poor |
| June 20 | Brieger Isaac | No Pass |
| Sept 2 | Berliner Benj | No Pass |
| Oct 2 | Bleichman Isidore | Disorder |
| 4 | Berliner Benj. | No Pass |
| 10 | Brown Louis | No Pass |
| 11 | Brown, Louis | No Pass |
| 2 | Bergman L. | Playing and talk |
| 16 | Brown Louis | No Pass |
| 18 | Brown Louis | No Pass |
| 30 | Bergman Louis | Disobedience |
| Nov 6 | Brown, Louis | No Pass |
| 9 | Brown Louis | No Pass |
| | Bergman Louis | Inattention |
| 22 | Bergman Louis | No Pass |

(above) A page from the HOA's Public School Detention Book and (left) the hand decorated title page.

(above, left) The former country home of John Jacob Astor, at York Avenue and 87th Street, served as the HSGS institution for girls from 1884 to 1888.

(far left) Homeless boys sleeping in an areaway were photographed by Jacob Riis in the 1880's. (From the collection of the Museum of the City of New York.)

(above) Bathing by the numbers at the Brooklyn Hebrew Orphan Asylum in 1899, and (below, left) at the Home for Hebrew Infants in 1905.

(above, left) Calisthenics for the youngest girls of the HSGS orphanage, Broadway at 150th Street, 1903, when clothing was bought in job lots and heads shaved for cleanliness.

(above) Hebrew Sheltering Guardian Society girls in their dormitory at the turn of the century.

(upper right) The BHOA's "House on the Hill" at Ralph and Howard Avenues, served Brooklyn orphans from 1892 until it closed in 1939.

(lower right) Girls in their playground at the HSGS orphanage, 1903.

(above) Meal time en masse in the dining room of the Brooklyn Hebrew Orphan Asylum, 1899.

(upper left) The Hebrew Orphan Asylum Military Band, 1906, was part of a musical training program established in 1868. The group often gave public performances, and won many prizes in band competitions, then popular.

(lower left) In 1902, when segregation of the sexes was strictly enforced, brothers and sisters met once a month at the HSGS orphanage.

(above) Social dancing at the Pleasantville Cottage School, 1912, is led by the cottage mother.

(above, right) Judge Gustave Hartman presides at a story hour in the early '20's at the Israel Orphan Asylum, later renamed the Gustave Hartman Home for Children in his honor.

(below, right) Dignitaries assembled for ground breaking ceremonies at the Pleasantville Cottage School, c. 1910.

# HOMEFINDER

## THE HEBREW SHELTERING GUARDIAN SOCIETY

**Home Bureau**

**470 West 145th Street**

Vol. 1. No. 1.          MARCH, 1922

## HELP US PROVE IT

"I want to live with a lady and a man as if they were my father and mother. I used to feel so ashamed when visitors came to "The Home" and looked us over as if there was something queer about us, so many in one place. It is so different to live with a family, to go to public school and be a part of the big crowd of school children, to see my father very often, to go to see all my aunts and uncles like others do, to play with the children next door, and the

(left) Mary Boretz, a crusader in the campaign to place children in foster homes rather than in institutions, was head of the HSGS Foster Home Bureau for more than twenty-five years.

(below) The final home of the Hebrew Orphan Asylum at 137th Street and Amsterdam Avenue, from 1884-1941. At its peak it sheltered 1,500 orphans.

(far left) The first issue of Mary Boretz's paper for foster families, 1922.

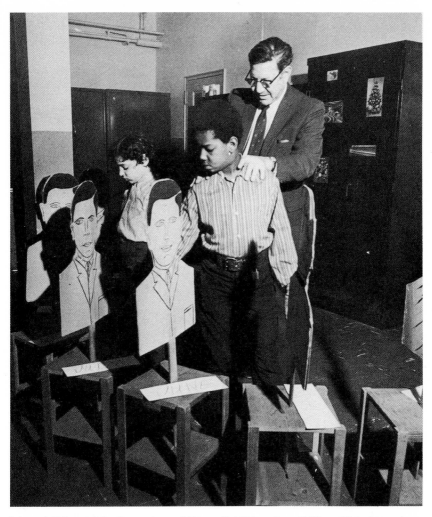

(above) Edenwald's Supervisor of Remedial Education, William Finkel, teaches a retarded child to understand the concept of "before" and "after."

(above, left) Finger-painting offers an opportunity for self-expression for youngsters at Childville, a treatment center for severely disturbed children.

(below, left) Dr. Sol Nichtern, director of the JCCA's Psychiatric Clinic talks with a foster child. Psychiatric help is available to all children in care.

Candice Love I-AM-HAPPY-HERE. I think-you for
#-LETTING-ME-GO-TO-MY-MOTHER.

THANK-YOU-FOR-TAKING-CARE-OF-ME.
THANK-YOU-FOR-THE-HEALTHY-FOOD.
THANK-YOU-FOR-BUYING-MY-BEAUTIFUL
-WATCH. -I-AM-TAKING-CARE-OF-IT.
-THANK YOU-FOR-TAKING-ME-
-EVERY-PLACE-YOU-WENT.


+CandiceLOVE

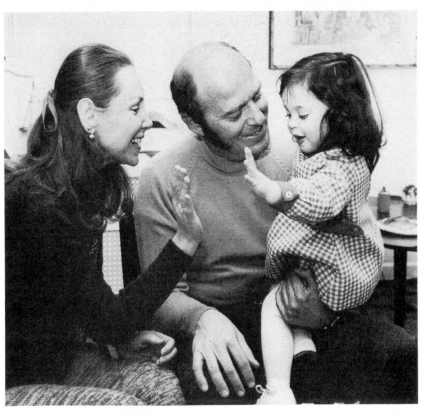

(above) A foster family enjoys a game of "pattycakes" with their foster daughter.

(left) The arms of a foster mother offer a little girl a moment of closeness.

(far left) A letter written by a foster child to her foster parents after returning to her own home.

(above) Children at the Pleasantville Cottage School in Westchester County enjoy a mid-morning chat in the rotunda with their counselor.

(above, left) The back yard patio of the Youth Residence Center on Manhattan's upper East Side is an informal meeting place for the forty adolescent residents.

(lower left) A friend's room is a good place to relax at the Friendly Home for girls, one of JCCA's twelve group residences.

Family Day Care Service was introduced to New York by the Jewish Child Care Association in 1952. Supervised family homes, recruited in the child's own neighborhood, care for 2-month olds to 3-year olds, too young for group care, whose mothers must work, or who are unable, because of physical or mental illness, to care for them full time.

administering the new Social Security measures that would help keep a home intact, the long psychological strain was breaking families apart. "There has been an increase in the number of children committed for foster care," warned the chairman of the Home Bureau Committee, Florence Stix, "and the problems they present are more acute."

It was a time of catastrophe and chaos throughout the world. During this same period the Hitler regime came to power in Germany, and problems more "tragic" than any American could imagine faced Europe's Jews. By 1934, many fearful German parents had read the handwriting on the wall. German-Jewish children, aged 12 to 16, were arriving in New York, sent away "until things improved" in their homeland. Because they needed foster care, the Jewish agencies were called upon to help.

With Herman Block as president and the Home Bureau and the HOA providing staff and consultants, the German-Jewish Children's Aid (later the European-Jewish Children's Aid) was organized in 1934. Caseworker Lotte Marcuse left Mary Boretz' staff to become the new agency's director of placement, and a national campaign was launched to find foster homes for children who had no relatives here to take them.

The first 105 children landed in 1934 and were temporarily sheltered at the reception houses of the various Jewish institutions until plans could be made for their care elsewhere. Sara Egelson left the HOA Boarding Out Department to escort the new arrivals to preferred homes as far away as California. In 1938, the Home Bureau itself arranged placement in New York City of 75 German children from 12 to 16 years of age.

It was in November of that year that the synagogues of Germany were burned to the ground by order of Hitler. There was no longer any question of a return home for Jewish children. Escape from the Nazis had become a matter of life and death. Some 600 refugee children reached the United States, under the auspices of German-Jewish Children's Aid, between 1934 and 1940. They were a handful of the millions in peril. Most of the other children were later to be destroyed in the death camps.

Many young Jewish adults also escaped the Nazi terror by fleeing to this country. Well-educated and resourceful, many had been professionals — teachers, lawyers, psychologists, musicians or social workers — in their homeland. A number came to Pleasantville, to the HOA and the BHOA in the thirties to work as cottage parents and counselors, enriching the lives of the children and the quality of the staff. Others joined the Home Bureau. Henry Selver later became assistant director at the Cottage School. Erika Juliusburger, Ida Freedman and Edith Bloch are today among JCCA's top foster home division administrators. Marie L. Laufer heads the Joint Planning Service which now handles intake for JCCA and the Jewish Board of Guardians. Bertel Gordon is administrator of the agency's innovative Family Day Care Service. Margaret Kahn for many years headed JCCA's central intake service, and was the first director of the Joint Planning Service, which succeeded it. All were emigres during the Hitler years. Germany's loss was the New York children's gain.

And then there was a young refugee lawyer named Werner W. Boehm whom Lionel Simmonds hired to serve as a counselor under Myron Blanchard at Edenwald. The young man became so interested in the field that he took graduate training in social work, and now is dean of the School of Social Work at Rutgers University.

With the increasingly disturbed children admitted during the depression years, foster home units and congregate institutions alike came to realize that the psychiatric and psychological services they provided were not enough. These children needed more than diagnosis and educational guidance; they needed treatment. But money for expanded services was hard to find in the thirties. For the foster home units in particular it began to appear grossly wasteful not to pool their assets and their services as had been urged as long ago as 1926 in the Federation-sponsored study of the Bureau of Jewish Social Research.

Financial pressure toward such a union had mounted since 1926. The depression had sharply reduced philanthropic sources of money. In some cases, services had had to be curtailed. By 1936, lack of staff and budget at the Home Bureau and the HOA's Boarding Department made for long delays in placing a child in a foster home. On more than one occasion the Home Bureau had to close its doors to new admissions for several months. At the HOA, children "recommended" to the Boarding Out Department sometimes waited eight or more weeks in the reception house. Neither foster home unit was willing to sacrifice the quality of its care by overwhelming its workers with unmanageable caseloads. Nor was it possible to find funds for additional personnel. In fact, staff members had suffered three pay cuts in a row.

Other pressures for other kinds of union, too, had grown. Union was in the air. With the encouragement of the Wagner Labor Relations Act, industrial workers, relief recipients, unemployed, welfare workers, and professionals—all had been organizing to improve their lives and their working conditions. The employees of the Federation agencies had formed a union—one of the first to include professionals—and, despite strong disapproval at the executive level, were pressing for a contract. (It was not until some years after the recommended merger of the major agencies had been consummated that union recognition on an agency-wide basis was finally achieved.)

Meanwhile, corporations all over the country had been combining forces to save themselves from extinction. Why not a merger of Jewish child care organizations to eliminate duplication of services and give better service at less cost?

It was no new idea either for philanthropy or child welfare. Fund-raising had been merged in 1917 when the Federation of Jewish Philanthropic Societies was started. A start had been made toward a merger of intake in 1922 when the Jewish Children's Clearing Bureau began "recommending" children to the different agencies. True, the various institutions and agencies still had the right to refuse a child and their representatives continued to battle over policies at the Clearing Bureau board meetings. But compromise could be reached when people met face to face — *year after year* — and faced up to hard facts.

Year after year, members of the Child Care Committee of Federation, patiently but persistently led by Herman Block, had pressed for further steps toward a merger of child care services. The studies conducted by the Bureau of Jewish Social Research had urged not only the combining of the foster home services but, in 1930, the creation of a committee to plan a merger of the HOA and the Hebrew Sheltering Guardian Society. Five successive

Federation presidents had given these recommendations the full support of their prestige. But by 1937, the results could still be characterized by Block as a "100% *battling* average."

Still, *something* was stirring. The first inter-agency discussion of common problems had come cautiously in March, 1933, at a conference on discharge policies and practices organized by the Bureau of Jewish Social Research. Soon sub-committees formed by personnel of the HOA, HSGS, Fellowship House and the Clearing Bureau were holding regular meetings and submitting yearly progress reports. A merger committee twice went so far as to consummate an agreement. Each time the boards of the two powerful institutions backed suspiciously away.

But the years of discussion at least served to ease the original hostility and mistrust. If, by 1937, relations were not "exactly cordial," as Herman Block put it, still they could be termed courteous. I. Howard Lehman, as president of the HOA, and Block, as president of the HSGS, were meeting with increasing frequency for lunch. What had been barely concealed antagonism now was affectionate bantering. But the HOA — the patriarch of the New York Jewish orphanages — still was finding it hard to contemplate giving up its autonomy.

It was no longer a question of "foster care versus institution." By the late thirties, even the HOA had conceded that a foster home was a better place than an orphanage for the average child, and this change in attitude was reflected in its practice. In 1916, the institution had had 426 children in boarding homes — awaiting transfer to the institution which, with 1,329 children, was full beyond capacity. By 1940, the HOA had 1,000 in boarding homes as a matter of planned policy and only 607 in "The Academy" as its children now insisted on calling it.

Across the East River, spurred by its former superintendent, Aaron Jacoby, himself a former ward of the HOA, the institution on Ralph Avenue had even more completely reversed its traditional policies. The studies of Dr. Lawson Lowery (a BHOA staff psychiatrist) and Dr. Lauretta Bender, in the late thirties, had convinced the last reluctant board member that huge congregate institutions could no longer be justified. Children needed individualized attention. By July 1, 1939, the BHOA — the third largest Jewish orphanage in the country — had transferred its last charge to a foster home and closed forever the doors of its huge "House on the Hill." As the Children's Service Bureau with new offices at 150 Court Street, it now operated solely as a foster home service.

But such decisions involved genuine sacrifice on the part of trustees. It was hard to contemplate giving up those visible and so satisfying proofs of the value of a philanthropic effort. The buildings, the well-kept children — all were there before your eyes.

Former HOA trustees still recall with nostalgia those days when trustees "were made of sterner stuff." "The superintendent commanded respect, but the trustees ran the institution," says lawyer Chester Rohrlich, who later became a president of JCCA.

Every Sunday, the board members drove up Amsterdam Avenue in their chauffeured Cadillacs and Packards — which, twenty years earlier, had been Packards and Pierce Arrows — en route to their weekly conference with the superintendent. There it stood, their imposing orphanage — as complete as a medieval town. With its engine room to generate its own electricity, its separate five-story hospital, its huge separate gymnasium, its carpentry shop, its shoe repair shop, its dental clinic, its barber shop, its tailor shop, its enormous laundry, its tremendous, beautifully equipped kitchen, its cooking school, its fragrant baker's ovens, its infirmary with sleep-in nurse, its caning shop, its huge playing field and beautifully landscaped gardens, its archives, its library, and an entire public school on the ground floor.

A merger between the HOA and HSGS undoubtedly would mean an eventual closing of one of the two institutions. Who would swallow whom?

For a while the idea of closing Pleasantville and building a merged cottage institution at Edenwald was discussed. But there were those other nagging questions. What board would dominate? What top professional staff would survive the merger and remain to carry out the plans?

Yet the plans themselves began to appear more and more tempting. What had seemed to some, at first, chiefly a question of saving money began to seem to all rather a matter of spending the same money to far better serve the children. At last it came down quite simply to this: finding a trusted mediator. If a mediator truly above all institutional disputes and rivalries could be found, the two boards would merge.

In 1938, the HOA's Lehman and the HSGS' Block decided they had found that man in an old friend of Block's, Dr. Maurice Hexter. Dr. Hexter had just returned from Palestine to serve as assistant to Solomon Loewenstein, at that time executive vice-president of Federation. Block's friend, it was agreed, had rich knowledge of the social services and experience as a negotiator. After 14 years as chief executive of Jewish charities, first in Milwaukee, then Cincinnati, and last Boston, he had served for ten years as American non-Zionist representative of the Jewish Agency in Jerusalem, in charge of colonization work in Palestine. For nine of those ten years, he had administered the Palestine Emergency Fund and during his Palestinian experience had tested his diplomatic skills on such hardheaded opponents as the British Cabinet, the Palestine Royal Commission and the Jewish Colonization Association. It was agreed he *might* be able to handle the even more delicate problem of merging the HOA and the HSGS.

One problem appeared solved. Next came the problem of a name for the agency about to be born. Someone suggested "Hebrew Orphans Guardian Society" as a happy compromise. Someone else pointed out that HOGS would look exceedingly awkward on the uniforms of a Jewish children's band. At last, the name "New York Association for Jewish Children" proved acceptable to all.

January 12, 1940, the Hebrew Orphan Asylum, with its Boarding-Out Department, its Edenwald School, and its camps; the Hebrew Sheltering Guardian Society with its cottage institution and its Home Bureau; Fellowship House, and the Jewish Children's Clearing Bureau—all gave up their separate identities and became the New York Association for Jewish Children. (In 1945, the name was changed to the present Jewish Child Care Association of New York (JCCA).) I. Howard Lehman was elected the new agency's first president and Herman Block gracefully took the post of vice-president. Dr. Hexter agreed to stay on as executive director for the first formative period.

Even before the ink on the merger papers was dry, the architects of the new children's agency had cast their net to draw in and transform another congregate institution. Up in the Bronx stood the Home for Hebrew Infants. For ten years the battle for the babies had been waged between the institution and the foster home proponents. Now that battle, too, came to a "boiling, broiling, sizzling" head.

# Chapter 8

# The Rights of Infants

*"But the early years, though forgotten, cannot be erased. No more than we can admire the full-grown rose and overlook the fact that it developed from a healthy bud."* BENNO NEUBERGER, PRESIDENT, HOME FOR HEBREW INFANTS, 10th ANNUAL REPORT, 1906.

O NLY THE POOR ABANDON THEIR CHILDREN," wrote Jacob Riis in 1890, five years before the Hebrew Infants Asylum opened its doors in the South Bronx. "In midwinter when the poor shiver in their homes, and in the dog-days when the fierce heat and foul air of the tenements smother their babies by the thousands, they are found, sometimes three and four in a night, in hallways, in areas and on the doorsteps of the rich, with whose comfort in luxurious homes the wretched mother somehow connects her own misery." In hard times the number of abandoned babies noticeably increased.

Few survived their desertion long. Of 508 babies received at the Infants Hospital on Randall's Island from various sources in 1890, according to Riis, 333 had died. But he estimated the mortality figure as closer to 90% for the 170 foundlings included in the Randall's Island count. Many had arrived already half-dead from exposure. Seventy-two were dead when picked up in the streets.

Of course, there were — even in 1890 — other possible "solutions" for the desperately poor parent than abandoning an infant. Some took out insurance policies on their infants' lives, in the half-certain knowledge the child would die, if not of malnutrition then of the contagious diseases that ravaged tenement neighborhoods. The sums involved were pitifully small. Three companies discovered that they had insured a million children at weekly premiums of five to twenty-five cents.

Another solution — that at least freed the parent to work —

was to place a child for a small fee in the care of a "baby farm." A few such establishments were registered and licensed by the Board of Health, as the law required. The rest were characterized by the president of the Society for the Prevention of Cruelty to Children as "concerns by means of which persons, usually of disreputable character, eke out a living by taking two or three or four babies to board. . . . They feed them on sour milk, and give them paregoric to keep them quiet, until they die."

More fortunate was the infant left in the crib standing just inside the door of the great Foundling Asylum of the Sisters of Charity. In earlier days, the crib had been placed outside at night. But it filled up too rapidly. With the crib inside, the foundlings could be kept down to 1,000 a year.

Or the infant might be given over to the equally honest care of the House of Industry run by the Five Points Mission — an "enormous nursery school with an average of more than 400 day scholars and constant boarders. . . . "

But these of course were Christian institutions. In 1890, no Jewish institution had facilities for a child under three, although the HOA and the United Hebrew Charities sometimes boarded out the tiny ones with a wet nurse. However, with the flood of Jewish immigration in the late nineteenth century, this no longer seemed adequate. Who knew how many Jewish babies were deposited in the crib of the Catholic sisters — forever lost to the faith of their fathers?

By 1893, wet nursing seemed a hopelessly outdated method of infant care to progressive-minded Jews. That year, a group headed by Mrs. S. Wallenstein started looking for a suitable building in which to start an up-to-date institution to care for Jewish children "under the age of five years, born in wedlock, whose parents through death or any other cause are unable to give them proper care." (At the time, although the policy later changed, the illegitimate Jewish child seemingly was left to the Catholics.)

Subscribers, members, and patrons were sought to finance the new venture, and all contributions for the work were gratefully accepted. The proceeds of a "Lemonade and Candy Stand" came from "Master Sidney Berlin and little Miss Gertie Davidson, both ten years old." One hundred dollars from Felix Warburg on the birth of a son; $250 from the proud grandpa, Jacob H. Schiff.

A handful of infants were boarded out for two years until, in 1895, the Hebrew Infants Asylum (briefly more modishly known as the Hebrew *Enfants* Asylum) opened in a spacious and airy house at East 149th Street and Mott Avenue. Surrounded by beautiful grounds, this first building had room for 34 children.

Five children moved in May 26. By the end of one year, 42 little infants had lain in the new white-painted iron cribs. Within two more years, the asylum, overcrowded, was forced to move. This time, the board found a pre-Civil War fieldstone manor house at 161st Street and Eagle Avenue in the Bronx, with room for 150 children.

The board, all of whose officers for the first few years were women, planned conscientiously for the welfare of its charges. After careful search, "competent and at the same time kind persons" were found to assist a woman superintendent. A "Kindergarterin" was employed with "beneficial results." And the very latest child care methods were introduced, under the supervision of a medical board and an attending physician who examined each child on arrival and regularly thereafter.

New arrivals were washed, vaccinated, heads shaved, bodies clothed in spotless gowns and the toddlers' feet shod in black, button-up boots. All infants received daily baths — some several a day with chemicals added to the water for medicinal purposes. In feeding, too, the very latest pediatric standards were adopted. The feeding was regulated, "in accordance with the tables of Prof. D. Escherich (Graz)," the milk sterilized "in accordance with the method of Dr. Sockolet of Munich," and the bottles closed "by means of the improved bottle caps (Dr. Stutz's invention)."

As in all other thoroughly modern children's institutions of that day, parents were grudgingly allowed a bare three hours with their child every first Sunday of the month. Parents did, in fact, present a constant threat of epidemic, especially terrifying in an institution for the very young, although blame was sometimes unfairly assigned. Thus an outbreak of measles that killed 14 infants in 1903 was mistakenly traced to a "careless mother" who was presumed to have introduced the sickness since her two children were the first to fall sick. In 1898, one superintendent had expressed her wholehearted sympathy with institutions which, because of the risk, limited parents to a quarterly visit.

This particular superintendent had just lived through an especially harrowing year. Scarlet fever had raged in the wards, throughout January, February and March. Measles had arrived in April and May, just in time to catch several infants on their return from the hospital where they had been confined with the first disease. January, in addition to scarlet fever, also produced several cases of mumps. And a number of children — including several nurslings only a few days old — had caught all three. But the year was not over! Before its end, scarlet fever had reappeared. Four routine cases of diphtheria also were reported, but, thanks to Dr. Schick's new anti-toxin, diphtheria was now easily controlled.

To complete the roster: pneumonia, intestinal obstructions and convulsions — all complicating measles — killed three children. The fourth death that year had been from scarlet fever. Given the conditions of the day, it seems a miracle of concerned care that, of 141 infants sheltered over the twelve month period, only those four should have died.

The State Board of Charities would have agreed. When it published mortality figures for five New York institutions, in June, 1899, it showed an average death rate of one and one-half children per 100 for the Hebrew Infants Asylum. The next orphanage in line lost 17¼ children for each 100 in care. And the institution with the highest death rate lost 40 of 100 children.

But the next year proved disastrous both for the Jewish infants and for their exhausted caretakers. According to the annual report of 1900, the 215 children cared for over the 12 month period were almost simultaneously attacked by chicken pox, diphtheria, whooping cough, and scarlet fever. Twenty-two — or a little more than one out of 10 — children died. An entire ward overflowed with little victims of croup and pneumonia, some of whom also suffered from whooping cough. Yet with a city-wide mortality rate of six and a half per 100 children under five, and 20 per 100 for babies under one, it probably still was safer to live at the HIA than in the slums. In January, 1902, the *New York Herald* reported that "children under five years constitute nearly one-half of the pitiful procession that day and night winds its way to the (morgue)."

But the worst killers of institutionalized babies were always the acute and chronic diseases of the digestive tract so common among babies fed on the newfangled bottle. Only later, as formulas improved, did the incidence of gastroenteritis in all infant institutions drop sharply.

Under such conditions, is it any wonder if reports to the Board from the HHI superintendent often read like messages of desperation tossed from a medieval fortress? Marooned in the asylum for months at a time, with only their assistants and the attending doctor for adult company, surrounded by ailing infants, and harassed by repeatedly mentioned difficulties in keeping competent help on minimal wages, the early superintendents rarely stayed more than a few years.

By 1904, an old problem reappeared. Like the other Jewish children's institutions, the asylum once more was overcrowded. Within 15 months, 95 Jewish children under five had been committed to Christian institutions and to Christian wet nurses for lack of space in the Hebrew asylum. This time the board purchased a property about the size of "80 city lots" at Kingsbridge Road and Aqueduct Avenue in the Bronx and there erected a three-story stone and brick building with room for 450 children.

The new facilities opened in 1910 made possible an even more exemplary medical program. The separate three-story reception building and hospital endowed by Ivan M. Stettenheim included a laboratory which a second generous endowment had fully equipped and furnished with a pathologist. By 1915, the lowest death rate in the history of the institution was attributed to the work of this laboratory and the thousands of microscopic examinations of nose and throat cultures and eye discharges it made possible.

In 1913, another isolation building — the only one of its kind in the entire country — was added for the reception of infants under one. There each newly arrived baby spent its initial period of isolation in one of a long row of glass-walled cubicles, under the constant scrutiny of the nurse at the far end. Each bright, sunny cubicle had separate ventilation and contained everything necessary for the care of that baby.

The medical staff by now included a resident pediatrician, a board of 15 specialists, and a nursing crew for the two isolation departments. The food was excellent. The place and the children spotless. It seemed the safest place in the world for a baby to grow up.

But was it?

Freud and those who followed him had firmly established the importance of a child's formative years. Did the aseptic physical care of the infants' asylum answer the needs he had expounded? The advocates of foster home care were convinced it did not.

Rumblings of criticism were heard soon after the Hebrew Infants Asylum in 1917 became a charter member of the new Federation. Like the other institutions involved it too now had to sacrifice its members and other fund-raising prerogatives and the total independence these assured. But even more difficult, after 1922, as a member of the new Clearing Bureau it found its procedures under the severe scrutiny of men and women like Herman Block, Alice Seligsberg, Irma Scheuer and Mary Boretz who were firmly opposed to institutional care for most children and, most especially, for young children.

On joining the Federation, the asylum had changed its name to the less institutional-sounding "Home for Hebrew Infants." Now the HHI continued to make one concession after the other. In 1924, it agreed to refer its children at four years rather than five to the Home Bureau. A year later, under continuing pressure — and probably influenced by the overcrowding of the Home and the consensus of child care experts — it dropped its age of discharge another year.

But there all progress stalled. The Home for Hebrew Infants would not lower its graduating age below three. It seemed to both board and staff inconceivable that a baby under three could thrive as well in the average Jewish foster home as it could with the superb physical care it received in the institution. Many of the babies' own parents agreed. How could babies be cared for without doctors and nurses in constant attendance?

But as a succession of tiny children who had passed their first three or four years in the institution came into the Home Bureau — and homes were found for them — the determination of the foster home people also hardened.

Lucille Lazar has described the typical HHI three-year old —

"unable to talk, except for a few unintelligible words; shuffling and dragging his feet, his jaw dropped in the vacuum of his expression; lacking even the elementary knowledge of the normal eighteen-month-old baby in the poorest home; completely apathetic, or else so desperate in his need for affection and attention that the average adult could not handle his problems."

Yet only the most passionate advocates of foster home care could believe that Jewish mothers would open their homes to tiny babies. Such a mother would fear becoming too attached. Even Jewish widowers who could pay boarded their infants in non-Jewish homes because no mothers of their own religion could be found.

But the Home Bureau was accustomed to doing the supposedly impossible. It waved the skeptics aside, set its collective jaw, and set out to prove it *could* find homes for babies. With very little luck. Three years later, only five widowers' babies under three were in Jewish foster homes.

"Why," pleaded the *Homefinder. "Why* do Jewish women refuse to board babies?"

Suddenly, the question was no longer a question. One does not think of epidemics as bringing improvement in the lives of dependent children. But now a whooping cough epidemic in March, 1929 did just that.

The epidemic forced the infants institution and all the city's temporary shelters to refuse new admissions. Only the Home Bureau kept its doors open.

The staff swung into action. Backed by a six-months grant from Federation, they alerted the foster mothers of the community to the emergency. They announced it in newspaper advertisements, broadcast it over the radio, spread it by word of mouth and through the *Homefinder.* By the end of the six-month period, 15 little babies under three were living in Jewish foster homes. And even the Home Bureau office had a brand new look. A shiny new baby scale, bottles and nipples, and a tidy little stack of layettes were now part of the equipment. And, from time to time, a car loaded with crib, carriage and high chair could be found parked outside.

In those six months, the Home Bureau learned much about

working with babies and their foster mothers. Even the most old-fashioned Jewish mothers had proved willing to absorb the wisdom of the government child care pamphlets. To the Bureau, every baby was an individual with a unique constitution and a unique capacity to react to his environment. The psychological development and emotional needs of the child were stressed just as much as the physical care.

Physical care had to be emphasized, too, of course. All the more, in those early years, to compete with the standards of the institution. At first, a nurse regularly visited each foster infant, along with the social worker, and was on call day and night. But babies in foster homes, it was soon discovered, didn't need *super* health care, just *sensible* care. For one thing they were not as exposed to contagious disease as children in institutions, and were far less prone to respiratory infections when they lived in a caring family.

In the midst of the Home Bureau's struggles and successes, the 1930 White House Conference on Child Health and Protection affirmed once again that foster home care was preferable to institutional care for children under three. The Jewish Board of Guardians, which, at the time, had a home for unmarried mothers, now began asking Mary Boretz to take some of its illegitimate infants. And Alice Seligsberg at the Clearing Bureau started a long campaign to persuade the board of the Home for Hebrew Infants to allow its unvisited babies — those whose mothers never came to see them — to be transferred to a home where they could have the daily care of a foster mother.

By 1932, with continuing support from Federation, the Bureau had placed 134 babies under two and had added a pediatrician to its staff. That year, a three-year grant from the New York Foundation enabled the Bureau to add 25 more babies to its regular caseload for each of the three years, and to launch an experimental project to develop professional practices and clarify concepts and policies for infant foster home care.

By the end of the three-year period, no one any longer questioned the Home Bureau's capacity to provide care for even the youngest infant, and Mary Boretz and her workers had gained a special reputation for working miracles with sick babies. They had developed a series of "temporary" foster mothers who were especially patient and loving nurses and could pull back to life a baby dying for lack of any incentive to live. Even the non-professional staff at the Department of Public Welfare now would sometimes beg a Bureau worker to take an especially frail baby "who'll die if she doesn't get a mother."

But despite the growing conviction on all sides of the superiority of foster family care for babies, the HHI board was not ready to close the asylum. "Where would a baby go if there was no foster home ready for it?" pleaded the chairman in a desperate last stand. "Is it better to send a Jewish baby to a city hospital rather than here, to the Home for Hebrew Infants?"

It was a genuine fear. And the institution was conscientiously trying to give its tiny wards better psychological care. It was plain that fifteen minutes a day on the rocking horse did not satisfy a small child's need for stimulation! The HHI added a psychologist to its staff, and the psychologist, Dr. Rowena Ripin, introduced a nursery school. This did seem to make the children talk and play more. And parents now could visit every Sunday instead of only once a month.

Of course, the nursery only reached the older children and many children were unvisited. But the latter was not the institution's fault.

Few of those in care by 1938 were "born in wedlock" and many unwed mothers could not or did not come to see their offspring. The institution compensated as best it could by providing volunteer visitors to inject some bit of maternal attention. But the professionals continued to criticize.

They pointed out that the pediatrician was the only man in the lives of all these children. That the institution was staffed only by nurses without psychiatric training — none of whom, in any case, had time to give individual care. Or that the children — except for those in the nursery school who had the use of a small back yard — never saw the world outside save through window glass. Never were the children taken for walks or excursions in the neighborhood for fear they might catch some germ. Nothing was done to prepare a child for the day a social worker would come with a car and transport the three-year-old to a foster home and a new world full of strange and terrifying demands.

The Home Bureau had long been aware of adjustment problems these children had in foster homes. Now even more disturbing reports began to circulate, based on three psychiatric studies in progress.

In the late thirties, HHI Superintendent Mary Creed visited the BHOA to hear Dr. Lawson G. Lowrey of the Brooklyn asylum's new psychiatric department discuss his study of the difficulties experienced by BHOA foster families in caring for children reared in the HHI. She anxiously reported the paper to her board as "a severe criticism of institutional care for infants of which the board should be aware."

During this same period, it became generally known that a young psychologist named William Goldfarb was conducting a similar study for the Home Bureau. But his research went further than Dr. Lowrey's. Dr. Goldfarb, who later became a psychiatrist and director of the Henry Ittleson Center for Child Research, was comparing — at different ages — children who had spent their first three years in the HHI with those whose infancy had been spent in a foster home.

The third study was underway at Bellevue Hospital. There Dr. Lauretta Bender had been observing former HHI children referred to the hospital's psychiatric division. All three researchers were reaching the same conclusions. And the conclusions were all damning.

The 28 children Dr. Lowrey studied had been brought to his attention because they could not adjust in any foster home in which they were placed. As a group, he found them hyperactive, hostilely aggressive, selfish, uncontrollable, and demanding of constant attention. Central to their problems seemed to be an insatiable need for affection with no ability either to accept or return whatever love they won. Seventy percent of the children in his sample had speech defects which he attributed, like other problems, to the "isolation factor" in the infant's early institutional life. Transferred from foster home to foster home, in a vain effort to find the "right" family, these children's problems seemed only to get worse.

Dr. Goldfarb's findings agreed with Dr. Lowrey's. He added

that the aggressiveness of the institutional children stemmed not only from a "greater absence of control" but from a "fundamental desire to hurt others." Overwhelmingly clear was the fact that these children, having experienced no love relationship as infants, had no capacity to build one. Many, in addition, were intellectually retarded.

Could children so damaged be helped? Dr. Bender's study of those sent to Bellevue for psychiatric treatment concluded they could not, at least not in any fundamental sense. She found those she studied "hyperkinetic and distractible; they are completely confused about human relationships, and tell of half a dozen mothers and fathers and say everybody is their brother and sister", but "they love only themselves and lose themselves in a destructive fantasy life directed both against the world and against themselves."

Follow-up studies *did* show that "some of these children finally settled down to a life in an orphan home (and) some were accepted by particularly understanding mothers," but "all remained infantile, unhappy and unable to adjust to other children or the schoolroom." Dr. Bender classified her subjects as psychopathic personalities and placed the blame squarely on emotional deprivation during their early formative years.

All three researchers agreed that the institutional children studied were classic cases of what Dr. David M. Levy earlier had termed "affect hunger" — a "state of privation due primarily to a lack of maternal affection, with a resulting need, as of food in a state of starvation."

Although the studies-in-progress and their emerging conclusions already were well known in child care circles by the late thirties, the papers quoted were not published until the forties. They proved a seminal influence in brightening the early years of uncounted children yet to come.

To those responsible for the diminishing number of children at the Home for Hebrew Infants, these reports were like nails hammered into the heart.

Oh, the institution *had* tried! Back in 1903, Superintendent Jennie Abarbanell had echoed Samuel Levy and Ludwig Bernstein's concern for "individualization." "If I were to be asked the most important element in the success of our work," she told the board, "I should reply 'careful and conscientious study of the children as individuals'. . . . The pedantic notion that one system of training and one system of diet will do for all children belongs to the dark ages of charitable work; it has no place here."

Brave and innocent words for the head of an infants' asylum that already at the time held 155 children. Nor could the superintendent who cheerfully reported three years later the children's affectionate manner toward strange visitors — "with their sweetly pathetic appellation of 'Mama' and 'Papa' " — have dreamed that 30 years later this unfocussed affection would seem merely pathological to experts.

At the suggestion of Federation, the institution had added a casework department in 1938 to meet some of the increasing criticism. When young Esther Simon — later associate executive director of JCCA — was hired as the HHI's first social worker, she found the hardworking, upright superintendent deeply hurt by the harsh comments she heard at every meeting of the Jewish Children's Clearing Bureau.

Mary Creed was a registered nurse, not a social worker. She told the new HHI employee: "They make us feel like murderers. But that's why we hired you."

The HHI board gave Miss Simon and her staff the go-ahead to plan for the babies from the moment of admission — to explore ways to move the children out of the institution into permanent homes as soon as possible — either through adoption or through an expedited return home. For most youngsters, average stay in the institution was much reduced.

The new caseworker found some of the children surprisingly well-developed. But, usually, these were children who anywhere in life would have attracted attention to themselves — the pets of any ward they might occupy.

There was no longer any real question. Miss Simon had only to corroborate the findings of the psychiatrists. When this was done, the Home for Hebrew Infants knew it had to close.

Preparatory to this, in October of 1942, the institution merged with the 34-month-old New York Association for Jewish Children.

# Chapter 9

# One From Many

*"This agency has stood and will continue to stand for growth that comes from divergence of thinking instead of agreement."*
MARY BORETZ, FOSTER HOME BUREAU, GENERAL STAFF CONFERENCE, SEPTEMBER 13, 1940.

THE TASK OF FORMING a single child care agency from the overlapping, competing, and sometimes obsolescent parts of five proved predictably difficult. It required all the firmness, tact and dexterity displayed during Dr. Maurice Hexter's former Palestinian negotiations. It called for the greatest diplomacy and willingness-to-bend on the part of the two former presidents of the largest of the merged agencies, I. Howard Lehman and Herman Block. And it took the better part of the next six years.

The 1940 merger — which did not include the HHI — had established a new association with impressive assets for carrying out a program of improved services to children. Material assets alone included buildings and equipment valued at over $3,000,000, scholarship and other restricted educational funds of more than $458,000, and additional restricted funds, securities, bonds, property and cash worth almost $1,600,000.

The agency owned the two-square-block HOA property on Amsterdam Avenue behind City College; the buildings and 95½ acres at Edenwald; 13 cottages, an administration building, and 175 acres at Pleasantville; and the house at 1646 York Avenue which had belonged to the Jewish Children's Clearing Bureau. The second merger, in 1942, added to this the land, buildings and substantial resources of the Home for Hebrew Infants.

The association's human assets gave even greater promise of a creative future. These included a dedicated and seasoned board, a pioneering professional staff, and the wholehearted backing of the city's Jewish philanthropic community.

As of January 1, 1940, this group found itself responsible for 3,471 children. Of those, 2,084 were in foster homes, 302 at

Pleasantville, 90 at Edenwald, 388 in Fellowship House aftercare — and 607 in the HOA "Academy."

One of Dr. Hexter's first goals was to scrap the obsolete services. The HOA Academy — the patriarch orphanage which, over 80 years, had cared for more than 18,000 children — had served its purpose. It was time to close. Quietly, Dr. Hexter went about making other provisions for the children.

Three years earlier, when the board of the Brooklyn HOA had made its historic decision to close that institution, one of the astonishing discoveries had been the number of families suddenly found able to take their children back. In 1940 and 1941, the caseworkers making plans for the children of the HOA Academy found history repeating itelf.

A tubercular widower had recovered his health since his son's original placement. An aunt suddenly had room for her niece. An older brother or sister had married and could accommodate just one more. Or a couple, helped by counseling or referral to a family service agency or the public aid program, found they were ready and able now to make a home for their two children.

Like its Brooklyn counterpart, the HOA — always subject to what Dr. Hexter labelled the "dastardly pressure to keep beds occupied" — had made little effort to keep in touch with shifting family situations. It left the initiative up to the parent or the review staff of the undermanned Department of Welfare. But the permissive visiting policies introduced in the twenties had narrowed the earlier gulf between wards and parents. Now 30% of the children were found able and happy to go home.

If someone had bothered to check sooner, might not the stay in the institution for many of these children have been greatly shortened? The average stay in the Academy in 1939 was five and a half years. Some had been there 10. At Pleasantville — which had started work with the families of children in placement in 1938 in a collaborative effort with Fellowship House — the average stay had been reduced to three and a half years. To Mary Boretz even that seemed too long.

Among the children most easily moved out of the HOA now were the older ones who had been maintained on the institution's "free list" well past the city-subsidized age of 16, while they completed their education. Arrangements could have been made for these, long ago, in boarding homes or at the Lavanburg Corner House. Now this was done. The majority of the others were transferred to foster homes. Some went to Pleasantville.

Last to leave the cavernous, almost empty structure were a group of 14 severely retarded children living on the top floor. The HOA had been trying for years, without success, to transfer them to the state institution at Haverstraw. Now at last they were accepted.

To the last, it proved painful for the former board members to face the closing of their famous institution. Dr. Hexter recalls I. Howard Lehman asking him, half-smiling: "But what will the board do without the children? We so much enjoyed going up there to play with them."

As a test of the board's real knowledge of the children's daily lives, Dr. Hexter asked a trustee how many mattresses were on the youngsters' cots.

"Since you inquire," came the reply, "I suppose it must be two rather than one."

He was wrong. Because of persistent enuresis, a problem endemic in all children's institutions, the cots had only an easily washed folded blanket instead of a mattress. But the point had been made, and was gracefully accepted: the former board members in fact knew very little of the quality of the lives of the institutional children.

By September, 1941, the last child was out. Seventeen months later, the entire two-block property was sold to the city for $1,344,000. In 1955, the buildings were torn down. Today the site is occupied partly by the Jacob H. Schiff School (P.S. 192 — the same number it carried when the HOA children were its students) and partly by a playground.

The emptying of the Home for Hebrew Infants started with an equal absence of fanfare in 1939, several years prior to its merger with the new agency. Here, too, parents were contacted by the new casework staff to see if they could take back their children.

Parents? Usually there was only a young mother. Sometimes no one. Most of the 250 children had been born out of wedlock.

Some of their mothers were in custodial care — mental institution or prison. Others had disappeared.

The mother who could be located was encouraged by the case-worker to explore her true feelings before reaching any decision about her child. She had three choices. If her clear wish was to set up a home for her baby, the worker could help her get assistance from welfare or from family service agencies.

Otherwise, the child could be placed in a foster home while the mother was helped to reach a decision. Her third alternative was to surrender her baby for adoption.

The process of exploring deeply buried feelings often took months. In the end, a surprising number of children went home with their mothers (who often still lived with *their* mothers). Many other babies were turned over to the Child Adoption Committee of the Free Synagogue (now the Louise Wise Services) which handled adoptions for the Jewish community. A few were transferred to foster homes, while a handful of mentally defective children went to the state institution at Haverstraw.

Some of the latter were already past their sixth birthday. The closing of the city institution on Randall's Island a few years earlier, had left the HHI with no place to send such children. Like the HOA, the infants' asylum had to wait years for the state to find room.

On April 2, 1943, the home closed its doors. It was the last of the nineteenth century congregate Jewish orphanages of New York. Today its buildings house the Kingsbridge Branch of the Home for Aged and Infirm Hebrews, the institution founded in 1870 by Priscilla Joachimsen, among others.

In 1947, the two HOA camps — Wehaha for Girls and Wakitan for Boys — also were closed. Even the critical Mary Boretz had classed these as "excellent facilities." But the new child care association preferred to follow the example of the Foster Home Bureau which, in 1939, had used 19 different Federation, scout and other camps for its charges. It was felt children in placement should not be segregated in the summer, but should have wider experiences with other children from the community.

A unified structure was essential for those divisions of the new agency which were to carry on. But not a structure so tight as to strangle the creative initiative and "divergence of thinking" that Mary Boretz and others hoped to retain. In 1939, in a report to Herman Block, Mary Boretz also had stressed another danger to avoid.

"Children's agencies in the past," she wrote, "have not been sufficiently sensitive to changing trends. It is important, therefore, to bear in mind that planning must include change."

Certainly, nobody could have stifled Mary Boretz's keen and compassionate mind. Her old friend, Herschel Alt, later for many years executive director of the Jewish Board of Guardians, has described the quality of that mind as "a total blend of professional interest and personal values." She was, recalls Dr. Hexter, "a wizard possessed of a driving daemon." Bedridden much of the time after 1927 because of a severe kidney ailment, often in great pain, she continued to head the Home Bureau for another 19 years. By that time she had left her indelible imprint on the field to which she devoted her life as well as on the agency she helped to shape.

She also left behind a trained staff and an educated board — both of a devotion rarely matched. "She expected devotion and dedication from her staff because she gave it. You never felt used by her," recalls Elizabeth Radinsky, director of the Jewish Youth Services of Brooklyn and later an associate executive director of JCCA, who worked with her for many years at the Home Bureau. "What she could do from her bed, no two of us with four feet could accomplish."

Every waking hour —"and because of her illness, that was many waking hours"— was spent thinking about the work and inspiring her staff with a dedication almost equal to her own. Phone in hand, surrounded by workers ("who *wanted* to go to her apartment," insists Mrs. Radinsky) she continued to exercise her leadership. Even in moments of great pain, she expected her secretary, Helen Sigman, to pass her papers and encourage her to get through the work.

Her forceful and patient interest in the education of board members helped several such as the late Dorothy Bernhard, later president of the Child Welfare League of America, and lawyer Helen Buttenweiser to become outstanding philanthropic leaders. (Both are granddaughters of Adolph Lewisohn). JCCA trustee

Katherine Stroock who worked with her as a young volunteer says simply: "She was a real guru."

Mary Boretz was among the architects and workers during the first years of the new agency's life. She retired as director of the Foster Home Bureau at the end of 1945, but continued as a consultant to JCCA and Federation and as a member of the executive committee of the Child Welfare League of America until her death, August 28, 1949.

Some of the early organizational problems that had to be resolved were obvious. The Jewish Children's Clearing Bureau was converted into a Central Intake Service to provide sole access to all agency units, and Evelyn Spiegel was appointed its director. The HOA and HSGS foster home units were merged into the Foster Home Bureau, still headed by Mary Boretz. Julia Goldman — after 16 years at Pleasantville, nine of these as the institution's head — was called back to the city to set up a Child Guidance Department. And a Youth Service Bureau was formed from the staffs of Fellowship House and the aftercare unit of the HOA, with Sarah Sussman still in charge.

The various consolidated services remained for some years dispersed around the city. (Ten years later, executive director Louis Sobel could still complain they behaved more like "compartments" than "departments," so difficult was it to sacrifice autonomy.) A central personnel director was not appointed until 1945, a public relations department was set up the next year. It was not until the agency moved into its present building at 345 Madison Avenue in 1960 that all the non-residential services were finally united under a single roof. It had taken 20 years.

The centralized personnel department, headed by Lucille Lazar, was over the years to play an important role in integrating the staffs of the merging agencies and in standardizing personnel practices. Almost immediately, the fledgling department was confronted with the thorny issue of labor-management relations.

The years following the merger had seen increased employee organizing activity and increased pressure for unionization. Board and administration found somewhat disconcerting the concept of a vertical union in a child care service ranging from social work professionals to maintenance workers. Nevertheless, by 1946, following prolonged negotiations, JCCA became the first of the city's child care organizations to accept unionization. An agency-wide agreement was signed by Chester Rohrlich, then president, and Charles I. Schottland, executive director, recognizing the Social Service Employees Union, United Office and Professional Workers CIO, as sole bargaining agent for JCCA staff.

The staff has continued to be unionized, but another union now represents JCCA employees — the Community and Social Agency Employees Union AFL-CIO, which also represent many other Federation and other social agencies. Labor-management negotiations have achieved agreement, despite turbulent periods, all but once in this quarter-century. (In 1964, there was a three-week strike against JCCA and the other Federation family and children's services.)

But the first visible result of progress resulting from merger, back in the forties, was a sharp reduction in numbers of children in care. From January, 1940 to July, 1943, the total number dropped by approximately one-third — from 3,471 to 2,059. This reflected the closing of the two large congregate orphanages with the return home of many children. It also reflected the many advantages of an intake department responsible only to a single agency.

Intake workers no longer had to contend with competing institutions and competing child care philosophies, all jockeying for children. Intake studies could be more thorough. Moreover, there were, by the 1940s, many more alternatives to placement for a family facing severe difficulties with a child. Family counselling services were expanding. So were child guidance clinics. Day care centers for children over 3 were common — at least during the war years. More homemaker services were available. And above all, the greatly expanded public aid programs of the New Deal were helping to keep thousands of the city's families if not comfortable at least alive and together.

By 1954, intake was the road to placement for only one-third of the Jewish families applying to JCCA. The other two-thirds had been helped to find less drastic solutions.

Among the 2,059 children remaining in JCCA care in July, 1943, were 152 Jewish refugee children from Europe who had been assigned to the agency by the European Jewish Children's Aid. This was a continuation of the emergency program started in 1934.

But the Jewish child refugees arriving in New York from 1940 to 1946 were far fewer than those who had come in the preceding six years. Only 375 were able to cross the ocean to freedom during the war. And they were far more scarred than the previous arrivals. Many had experienced life in the crowded detention camps of southern France and had seen their parents deported to Germany before crossing the Spanish border.

In the spring of 1946, however, the flow speeded up again, 750 young people landing within the first 16 months. Again the group's characteristics had changed. These were older — the majority over 17. Younger children had not survived the holocaust.

Mostly from Eastern Europe, the postwar Jewish refugee children were often the sole survivors of families whose deaths many of them had witnessed. Virtually all had been in one or more concentration or labor camps, or had lived for years like animals in the woods. A few had fought with partisan bands. After the war, they had wandered the roads of Europe until they came to the UNRRA camps.

Suffering from malnutrition, sometimes physically scarred, always emotionally scarred, some of the postwar refugees were placed at the Pleasantville Cottage School. Headed since 1944 by Jacob Hechler, the institution had developed the treatment services, experience, tolerance of deviant behavior and skilled staff to help many kinds of troubled children.

An even larger number went into foster homes. In a study of 46 of these, Paul Steinfeld, Pleasantville's present director, who at the time was a staff caseworker, noted their "amazing resistance" to their grueling experiences. Since they had lost from four to seven years of schooling, it was fortunate that they also had a "zeal for education."

JCCA and other agencies which have since merged with it undertook placement of hundreds of Jewish refugee children in New York during the war and postwar years. They went into JCCA foster homes, to Pleasantville, a few to Edenwald, some to group residences opened in the forties, some to the Hebrew National Orphan Home, others to the Jewish Youth Services of Brooklyn (former BHOA). The peak year for the JCCA alone was July, 1946 to July, 1947, when it served 430 young refugees — 19% of its total caseload.

One hundred and thirty-nine of these were receiving help through the Youth Services — which provided medical, dental, psychiatric, and educational or scholarship aid as well as foster homes where necessary. Two hundred and ninety-one were in the care of the Foster Home Department. (Sometimes the homes were free homes provided by relatives, but the children still required counseling and other services.)

Many of the young refugees helped went on to successful careers. Prominent among these is Dr. Fred Manasse, now a professor of physics at Dartmouth College, who entered the agency's care in 1945 with his brother, Gustav, now a clinical psychologist. Fred was 9½ at the time, Gustav 13. After their parents had arranged the boys' escape from Germany in 1939, the two had fled for six years across Europe — from institution to institution — until they reached Spain.

Understanding and affectionate care were needed to heal the fear and anger of those six years — particularly for little Fred. And understanding and affectionate care were finally found in a JCCA foster family. Despite his language and schooling handicaps, Fred graduated from Brooklyn Tech at 16½ with a record described as "outstanding" and, with the help of a JCCA board and maintenance scholarship, earned a "magna cum laude" from CCNY four years later. A Bell Fellowship was the award that later helped him complete his doctorate.

But caring for young victims of the holocaust was only one strand in the agency's history during the forties and early fifties. There were always crises to meet! One that confronted the agency in the mid-forties was the severe postwar shortage of foster homes, in part caused by the baby boom that emerged in the wake of the war. Jewish children now sometimes languished for seven to ten months in the crowded, understaffed city shelters for lack of an available foster home. It made some wonder if the HHI board had not been quite right in its fear that the institution would be missed.

In 1946, with an original investment of $85,000, the Jewish Child Care Association set up a small nursery expressly designed to spare babies and toddlers this traumatic experience. The idea was to combine the efficiency and lower per-capita operating cost of an institution with the warmth and individual attention a baby would get in a family.

A child admitted for shelter was not necessarily awaiting long-term placement. Perhaps intake was studying the case while considering what would be best. Or perhaps a mother suddenly was taken ill and there was no willing relative or long-term homemaker available.

Before the first year was up, the agency's error was plain. Despite the new facility's small size, the babies were not getting the love and stimulation every baby needs to grow into a caring and responsive adult. The only answer was to close the nursery down.

It was the first test of the new agency's courage to admit its own mistakes and to correct them. As Louis Sobel put it in 1954, "Experimentation requires not only readiness to move forward, but to move back when necessary."

The misbegotten nursery was replaced with a Temporary Shelter Care Program to provide temporary foster homes for Jewish children of all ages, if necessary on an emergency basis. It proved a struggle to find such homes. But a stubborn task force, headed by one of the first Home Bureau workers, Luba Joffe, accomplished this — greatly assisted by the decision to pay a special extra stipend. The Shelter Care Program was approved by the Department of Welfare, in October, 1946. From that time on, the agency followed a rule rarely broken: no Jewish child was to spend even one night in a public shelter.

The search for homes for babies in the forties was somewhat eased by the "prospective adoption" program pioneered by Mary Boretz during the preceding decade. Many more mothers would open their homes to a baby they could hope to adopt than to one they knew they would one day have to give up.

The program had started almost as soon as the Home Bureau began placing babies in 1929. From the very first Mary Boretz had pressed for the right to find permanent homes for those who became eligible for adoption while in care but whose backgrounds made them questionable candidates for adoptive placement, at least by the rigid standards of that day.

At that time, the Child Adoption Committee of the Free Synagogue (now Louise Wise Services) handled adoption services for the Jewish community. According to its then more traditional standards the "adoptable" child was one free of hereditary mental or physical taint, and whose physical, emotional and intellectual development was judged "normal."

By these measurements, many of the Home Bureau's otherwise adoptable babies were indeed dubious gambles. How certain could one be of the heredity of an out-of-wedlock child whose father was unknown and whose mother had disappeared or was confined to a mental institution?

Both Mary Boretz and Lucille Lazar, at the time assistant director of the Home Bureau, profoundly believed that these children, while they might have some problems, had every child's right to secure family ties. They knew, too, the importance of permanent placement for a child as early as possible, since stable family ties in early childhood were vital to emotional health.

Supported by its enlightened board, the bureau therefore developed in the early thirties a program of "prospective adoptive homes." An infant with no "strong or constructive" family ties could be placed in such a home on a regular boarding basis—with the foster parents' understanding that the placement might — or might not!—end in adoption. Even when legal adoption ultimately proved impossible, because the child's real mother could never make up her mind to surrender or because other barriers intruded, the extra interest and investment of many foster parents in a child that was "almost" theirs usually resulted in the de facto absorption of that child into the family.

A major problem remained. By community agreement and custom, only the Child Adoption Committee had the right actually to place a Jewish child for adoption. This meant that a child who after a few years in a "prospective adoptive home" proved to be adoptable could be removed from that home and placed in one the committee considered better.

To resolve this problem, the Home Bureau, on May 10, 1938, obtained the long-sought approval from Federation and the Department of Public Welfare of the agency's right to arrange adoptions for such children. Up at the Home for Hebrew Infants, young social worker Esther Simon set to work identifying the unvisited babies and sending them to the Home Bureau for prospective adoptive placement. By 1947, over 100 "unadoptable" babies had been adopted by foster families with whom they had been placed in this way.

Not every case worked out successfully, however. There were always a few where legal relinquishment could not be obtained — with deep sorrow to foster parents. And a few placements which were mismatches — harder for foster parents to accept when prospective adoption was in question.

In 1948, accordingly, the agency modified its policy — and abandoned the prospective adoption program. Young children thought to be possibly adoptive continued to be placed with foster families whom the staff felt might have the wish and the capacity to adopt — if and when. But the child was not identified to the family as a "prospective adoptive" until actual surrender was clearly in prospect.

On August 1, 1947, Louis H. Sobel, a former executive of the American Jewish Joint Distribution Committee, was appointed to head the Jewish Child Care Association. In his first annual report, Mr. Sobel stated:

"As a voluntary agency, we have a basic responsibility for study and research, for experimentation and demonstration. These functions have long been recognized as the most important contributions that voluntary agencies can make on the social welfare scene."

The next 25 years under Mr. Sobel and his successors would be years of struggle to meet that community obligation.

# Chapter 10
# Opening Doors

*"I am firmly convinced that the persistent factor in this story of steady growth in plant, personnel, and program is the spirit of dissatisfaction—dissatisfaction with anything less than the best within our realistic power to provide."* LOUIS H. SOBEL, EXECUTIVE DIRECTOR, JEWISH CHILD CARE ASSOCIATION, IN ANNUAL REPORT, 1949.

THE BROAD PRINCIPLES of present-day child care had by 1947 been developed and generally accepted. But implementing those principles still posed horizonless challenges.

A child's home was the best place for that child — if the home could be salvaged. But the challenge was no longer destitution. Families could hold *physically* together on Social Security survivors' benefits, welfare, aid to dependent children, and unemployment insurance. Now the challenge was psychological. How does one rehabilitate the emotionally disrupted family which by that time was the characteristic one referred to JCCA? And what were the criteria that indicated that a home could be rehabilitated?

The second best place for most young children is a foster home. But where is the dividing line between the child who can be cared for in this way and the child who will not be able to adjust? What intermediate forms of care — not a foster home, not yet a residential treatment center — can be devised for those children who straddle the line?

The final choice in placement — recommended only for the child who cannot be cared for in a community setting — is the residential treatment center. What further refinements could be developed to make that institution even more helpful to the increasingly disturbed children entrusted to it? How could their return to their families and to the community be speeded and eased?

A long road had been traveled since 1909 in the struggle to implement the principles first nationally proclaimed that year at the White House Conference on the Care of Dependent Children. The further possibilities, the endless subtleties, continued to stretch into the distance like a dream of infinity, every opening door revealing a further door. The last 25 years of the JCCA's effort have been spent opening those further doors.

The old Home Bureau had proved that many children suffering from cardiac conditions, diabetes, and other chronic physical ailments could effectively be cared for in foster homes. In 1949, the agency resumed its efforts to stretch the boundaries of foster home care and include even more seriously handicapped children.

Why, for instance, could not the very young severely disturbed child — the child between three and eight — benefit from placement of this kind? With the help of a generous gift from the Junior League for the Pleasantville Cottage School, an experiment — the Special Service Foster Home project — was launched with 8 small children. Some of these had been diagnosed as schizophrenic. Their only alternative to foster home placement in 1949 would have been a state hospital, if indeed any would accept children so young.

Instead, families were found who possessed unusual tolerance for bizarre and demanding behavior. Aware that they were part of a special project team, the families were given intensive support by the caseworker who, in some cases, visited or called almost daily to guide the foster mother. A special supplementary board rate was paid to mark recognition of the extra time, care and patience required. The child who could benefit received psychiatric treatment, several times a week. In a few cases, a special private nursery or school was also included in the plan.

The challenge of caring for children so disturbed proved a difficult and expensive one to meet. The day-to-day stress was heavy for foster parents and caseworkers. Improvement comes slowly to a schizophrenic youngster. Nevertheless, in 1955, the program was judged a success and extended to more children of this age and degree of disturbance.

There were other children who seemed to require an altogether new type of foster home facility. These were children who would benefit from remaining in the community but who, for various reasons, could not successfully be placed in a foster home.

There was eight-year-old Anna whose immature, unstable parents repeatedly undermined her placement with a substitute family.

And eleven-year-old Billy whose close ties to his own mother made him fiercely reject a substitute. And nine-year-old Sarah whose impulsive behavior and fear of intimate relationships presented an impossible problem to even the most tolerant of foster parents. And Leon. Leon had educational needs that required the specialized high school facilities only available in the community. But because the boy could not cope with the demands of a one-to-one relationship, he had to remain at Pleasantville.

In 1953, with the help of a three-year $50,000 grant from the Greater New York Fund, the JCCA launched another demonstration project to try to take care of these. It purchased a comfortable house in the Midwood section of Brooklyn, furnished it, installed a pair of foster parents ready to care for six atypical youngsters — and opened the first of its "agency-owned foster homes."

A cross between a group residence and a foster home, the experimental unit was designed to dilute the intimacy of normal family relationships while providing the warmth of a family atmosphere. Sharing with five other youngsters of varying ages diminished the intensity of their relationship with the adults in the home. It was a real home — but it was not just the foster parents' home. For troubled children, some rejected by previous foster families because of personality and emotional difficulties, a feeling of security could better be established here.

The caseworker and foster parents encouraged the children to see the agency itself as an unchangingly secure and protective presence. "Just as the agency brought you here, so they brought us to live here," one foster mother told a new boy.

"Objecting parents," too, felt less threatened and rivalrous. Another important advantage was the ease with which brothers and sisters could be placed together.

The agency-owned foster home turned out to be a unique and truly useful facility. A second home was purchased in 1956; an agency-rented apartment opened in 1969.

Projects like the special service foster homes and the agency-owned homes increased professional recognition of the potential among foster parents. Adequately selected, prepared and counselled, they could serve exceedingly difficult and handicapped youngsters with sensitivity and understanding and often extraordinary acceptance. But recognition in the form of adequate board rates, broader public understanding of the vital service they perform, and development of in-service training programs has been a slow process.

True, there had been a notable change from the early Home Bureau days when foster parents received a board rate of $18 monthly. By the 1950's, basic board rates had increased five-fold; supplementary allowances (for clothing and other needs) and services had increased proportionately. A study of foster home recruitment in 1955 showed that foster parents themselves were a prime referral source. In the curious spiral development characteristic of agencies, as well as of people, JCCA returned to and expanded an earlier model — the Foster Parents Group of Mary Boretz's day, a program which had gradually vanished. A new staff member — Bessie Schick Freed (succeeded some years later by Esta Gluck) — was engaged to organize a foster parents group and to develop a broad activities program, whose chief goal would be stimulation of recruitment.

The Foster Mothers and Fathers Committee proved helpful, as expected. Its value went further than recruitment. The meetings promoted an exchange of experiences helpful to foster parents. And the feedback of suggestions and problems regarding agency procedures and policies proved valuable to the agency. Agency-wide meetings and workshops were held for foster parents on issues of general concern, and a series of in-service training groups set up, many in outlying communities. A public relations program was also undertaken to intensify the effort to erase the tenacious image of "boarding homes" — the heritage of the grim old days — and to win public recognition for foster parenthood. That the effort has met with considerable success is shown by the character and status of the families who now offer themselves.

Just as the nature of the children coming into placement has changed, so have the foster families who serve them. The first-generation immigrant mothers of the early days — with "old country" ideas and limited education, usually working class and often with limited expectations for their foster children — have gradually given way to second- and third-generation New Yorkers. These are usually middle-class, more and more often suburban, college or high school graduates, and sometimes professionals, with lively aspirations for children and foster children, a keen awareness of opportunities — and not infrequently, an unusual capacity to work with professionals in helping troubled children.

Today the agency has broadened its in-service training program for foster parents, and raised its basic board rates (a city-wide foster care agency step) to $125 to $145 monthly, plus of course medical and dental care and allowances for clothing and other expenses. The number of those receiving supplementary rates for the care of handicapped or severely troubled children has increased. But the question of further professionalization of the foster parents' role remains open. It is waiting in the wings.

The possibilities of new kinds of community-based group residences to meet the special needs of children in need of placement were not exhausted by the agency-owned foster homes. Another type of facility soon was created, whose roots lay in the past.

The old orphanages had had their group residences for older adolescents. The HOA, its Cornerhouse for Boys and its Friendly Home for Girls. The BHOA, its Girls' Club. These residences had a simple purpose: they were halfway houses to help "normal" young people, discharged from the institution but without family to return to, while they finished school or started work and learned to adjust to independent life in the community.

By 1947, the agency had two such facilities. The Friendly Home for Girls was a spacious apartment for eight girls on Manhattan's Upper West Side. It had been operated independently by the Ladies Sewing Society of the former HOA until 1945 when that society had consolidated with JCCA. In 1947, another consolidation — with the Wayside Day Nursery on East 20th Street — had provided a three-story brownstone building, which JCCA remodelled into a residence for adolescent boys called Fellowship House.

But by the early fifties, it was more than apparent that halfway houses did not fill the need of the emotionally vulnerable children leaving Pleasantville or Edenwald. Those who could not return home — nor yet establish a home of their own — needed not just a halfway house, but an especially structured therapeutic environment to continue the gains made in placement and provide the emotional support essential to their adjustment in the community.

And what about those adolescent girls and boys who had never been in placement with the agency but whose problems were making it impossible to live with their own families? Was it not the agency's responsibility to provide for these, too?

In seeking answers to these questions the JCCA went on to experimentation that made it a leader in the use of specialized group residences for many kinds of troubled children.

Fellowship House was transformed into a small residential treatment unit for 16 troubled older boys who, with extra help, could adjust to work or study in the community. In Brooklyn, the Girls' Club, which had merged in 1948 with the Children's Service Bureau (BHOA) to form the Jewish Youth Services of Brooklyn, underwent parallel transformation. Marie Laufer who came there as the residence's first on-premises caseworker in 1949 recalls the difficulties in changing the old program.

There were 80 young women living in the overcrowded residence when she arrived. Some of these were as old as 28. There had never been any system for helping them move on. Often their dependence on the Club had been further accentuated by well-meaning workers who encouraged a break in their already frail family ties.

Marie Laufer, on the contrary, emphasized working with families to resolve conflicts. She aimed both at preservation of ties and freeing the youngster to grow and move on. Through casework and planning with youngsters and counseling with families, she managed within one year to reduce the Club's population to 30, aged 16 to 21. For the first time in years, most of the residents now could have private rooms.

As always in the past, change did not come easily. To a woman, the concerned board members were convinced the new caseworker was "not being nice enough to the girls." They feared the institution was withering away. But as the new program developed, with obvious benefits to the remaining young women, the board relinquished its doubts, and, in 1954, appointed Marie Laufer director.

In 1960, when the Jewish Youth Services of Brooklyn merged with JCCA, the Girls' Club joined the Manhattan-based agency. In November, 1968, both the Girls' Club and Fellowship House for Boys — their buildings no longer adequate nor suitable — were replaced by the new JCCA Youth Residence Center, an especially designed innovative residential treatment center on Manhattan's Upper East Side. The new center is one of the few coeducational treatment facilities in an open setting for this age group. It serves 20 young women and 20 young men, from 16 to 22, who live in separate wings but share dining, recreational, and other living facilities. The coeducational aspect, a vital feature of the therapeutic setting, was adopted on the advice of psychiatric consultants who felt that development of relaxed relationships with the opposite sex was an essential need of troubled youth.

While the two larger half-way houses were developing and merging into a single coeducational residential treatment center, JCCA was pioneering a totally new kind of group facility. The Friendly Home apartment became the first of a series of small group residences that are neither modified foster home nor converted halfway house but provide an open yet protected setting geared to the problems of the children living there.

At first these small community-based group residences were used exclusively for the teen-ager of normal intelligence. But their combination of freedom and controls with therapeutic help proved so uniquely valuable that the program, under the direction of Irving Rabinow, JCCA's first Group Residence Division director (now associate executive director), was extended to younger children and to children with other kinds of problems.

Today the agency has twelve such facilities located in the city and in Westchester. All are spacious apartments or attractive private houses, indistinguishable from the dwellings around them.

Nine of these, like the agency-owned foster homes, serve children not able to adjust to family life or those with "objecting" parents who prevent their placement in a foster home. But instead of foster parents, the units have salaried child care workers in charge — sometimes, but not always, a married couple. Four of the nine joined the group residence division in 1962 when

Hartman-Homecrest consolidated with JCCA. Two of these, located in suburban houses, are co-ed, serving 17 to 21 boys and girls, 8 to 14 years old. The other seven serve 8 adolescents from 15-18 — either boys or girls.

The three remaining and newer residences are unique. One serves 8 teen-age retarded boys, most of whom are graduates of the Edenwald program. The second, the Vernondale Group Residence, was opened in July 1971, to serve 8 severely orthopedically handicapped boys and girls who no longer need to live in a hospital but cannot go home. The facility was planned in cooperation with the Blythedale Children's Hospital, where some of the children — particularly those in wheelchairs — go to school and receive rehabilitative help. The Vernondale facility is thought to be the first group residence of its kind in the child welfare field. Typical of the children served was the first child admitted in 1971. A bright, motherless, seven-year-old boy with severe cerebral palsy, he can hold a pencil only between his teeth and is able to move about only in a special walker.

The third new group residence was opened in the spring of 1972, in a joint effort with the Jewish Family Service, to meet yet another area of community need — service to the young runaways attracted to the city in growing numbers in recent years. A ten-room apartment on the East Side, the residence is equipped to care for 10 girls and boys, 14 to 18 years old.

Working with JFS' Youth Emergency Service (YES) — a store-front service to youth in the East Village — the new residence differs markedly in several respects from other JCCA units. It is, first, a short-term facility with a time limit for residents of up to two weeks. And second, its staff of caseworkers and child care counselors includes "indigenous" workers — young people whose own life experience helps them to relate to troubled youth and to win their confidence.

The goal is to offer early intervention and effective help as quickly as possible, at a time when the young runaway is highly vulnerable to the exploitation of toughs who now frequent the area. Youngsters are offered intensive services during their brief stay; help in reuniting them with their own families or in planning a reasonable alternative; help in securing jobs; and medical and other treatment services.

In 1964, Martin Gula, Specialist on Group Care at the United States' Children's Bureau, summed up both the goals and the achievements of JCCA's group residence program: "In our country, the Jewish Child Care Association of New York has been a foremost leader, not only in developing its group residence program, but in using these resources in a refined and differentiated way as part of total agency development."

Today similar residences are used by voluntary agencies throughout the country to serve many special needs.

Perhaps the major problem that engaged the JCCA's "spirit of dissatisfaction" after 1950 was the effort to prevent placement — the search for more and better ways to help a child and family without having to remove the child from the home. Or failing this, the search for better ways to speed family rehabilitation and reunion.

Separation — the breaking up of the family involved in the very act of placing a child — had come more and more to be recognized as a traumatic experience for all involved. Most applications for placement now resulted from the emotional problems of parent or child, and this kind of separation, as Louis Sobel noted in 1954, "with its implication of disturbing differences and actual rejection" were even harder for a child or parent to accept than had been the common nineteenth century causes. Death, tuberculosis, mental breakdown and destitution had been visible facts of life. They seemed then unavoidable misfortunes for which no one could be blamed. But the diagnosis of emotional problems today suggests *someone* is at fault.

"Even under the best of circumstances," wrote Sobel, "separation is a process heavily charged with feelings of guilt, hurt, and hatred both for parent and child."

In the early fifties, JCCA began to experiment with an additional tool to avoid this trauma. The tool: family day care for children under three.

Children this age were too young for the group day care centers whose growth was stimulated during World War II and which served youngsters from three up. Those under three needed the more individualized care a motherly woman could provide in her own home. But nowhere in New York was such a program available under professional supervision.

Yet family day care was not new. Pioneered in Philadelphia in 1928 by the First Family Day Care Association, its introduction in New York had been urged by Alice Seligsberg at meetings of the Jewish Children's Clearing Bureau in the thirties and, not surprisingly, attempted by Mary Boretz on a small scale in the early forties. But the project needed more staff and funding than could be spared for it at that time. Now the upward trend of woman workers that had continued into the postwar era accelerated the need for such care.

In a preliminary study of the need, the New York Jewish Child Care Council headed by Edna Baer discovered that the Department of Welfare had received 524 requests for day care of babies under three during the last four months of 1951. An additional 100 requests had been reported by six group day care centers in Manhattan and Brooklyn. One temporary shelter reported that 13 children this age had been placed in shelter institutions over the past year only because their mothers had no place to leave them during the day. Four of these children had continued into long-term foster home placement. Couldn't that have been prevented?

It was clear that family day care could serve an important function beyond that of practical preventive to immediate foster care placement. It also could protect youngsters in their crucial early years from the hazards of unsupervised arrangements and enrich their development while enabling their parents to maintain independence.

In swift response, JCCA and the Jewish Youth Services of Brooklyn made the decision to move for the first time into day care, with the support of Federation and the able collaboration of Martha Selig, consultant on Child and Family Services. Under the persuasive leadership of administrator Elizabeth Radinsky, JYSB's director (later associate executive director of JCCA), an experimental project was launched in September, 1952, for 15 children between 8 months and 3 years of age. (Older siblings also were eligible if no nearby group care was available.) Individual care was provided from 8 a.m. to 6 p.m., five days a week, in family homes recruited in the child's own neighborhood.

Not only the child of a low-income working mother or father or of one struggling to continue education or training was eligible. Equally welcome was the child whose emotionally troubled parent — in therapy or just back from a mental hospital — needed partial relief from the stress of child care. All these small children needed the security of a day in a warm, relaxed home screened and supported by casework services. Their mothers as urgently needed the assurance that their children were safe and well cared for, at a fee within the limited family budget. Many also needed the help of the caseworker in coping with their own and their family's problems.

When the Eisman Day Nursery joined the project as co-sponsor in July, 1956, with a contribution of $30,000 for a two-year period, 15 more children were added. By 1962, the program was serving 65 children.

As the first such project in the state, the Family Day Care Service in 1961 received a special award from the New York State Welfare Conference for establishing a new pattern of child care services. No public funds were provided, however, until 1967, when new federal funding made available subsidies for family day care. When the city then set up its own program for babies and toddlers, Family Day Care Service was asked to organize training seminars for city workers. By January, 1972, the agency had 180 children in family day care, while eight other agencies in the City were providing similar services.

Other JCCA preventive services were being developed during these years. The Tri-Agency Project, financed by the Greater New York Fund, was launched in 1954, with the collaboration of the Jewish Family Service and, once more, the Jewish Youth Services of Brooklyn. The project was an experiment to prevent placement where the family applying was felt to have the strengths to remain together if prompt and adequate casework services were made available.

The family agency agreed to set up a special unit to provide immediate service to all clients referred from the two child placement agencies, while a committee representing all three would meet regularly to evaluate progress.

Valuable insights were gained through this project, which was renamed the Bi-Agency Project after the merger of JCCA with JYSB, and is now an ongoing program. With experience, criteria have been sharpened for adapting casework methods to these families in crisis. Underscored over and over was the need to be prepared to offer homemaker and other practical services.

As time went on, the Bi-Agency program also proved useful in serving another important agency goal — the acceleration of family reunion once a child was in placement. If a family was seen as being a promising candidate for reunion with intensive casework help, that family could be referred to Bi-Agency. Aftercare for such a family was part of the plan.

An incidental boon to the Bi-Agency effort to preserve families was the Department of Welfare's decision, in the late fifties, to reimburse agencies for homemaker services provided as an alternative to placement. This made it possible to spare many children uprooting into shelter care in a family emergency.

As the JCCA program developed in the fifties, it became more and more obvious that the "Child Guidance Department" set up at an earlier date was inadequate to the increasingly sophisticated needs of the agency. Although establishing the department had symbolized the general acceptance of a therapeutic responsibility for the children, the actual therapy was conducted by a panel of psychiatrists who saw the children in their private offices. The department merely administered the panel program, allocating a child to a psychiatrist and making appointments. The children were treated apart from the agency. Each division had its own psychiatric consultant (including Dr. Lillian Kaplan for the Foster Home Bureau and Central Intake, and Dr. David Beres for Pleasantville). Able as the individual consultants were, there was inadequate coordination.

At the same time, JCCA was developing an integrated treatment philosophy. But with 30 autonomous psychiatrists in various parts of the metropolitan area actually carrying out treatment, the agency had little control over treatment goals. The panel system could not provide a truly integrated program.

In 1955, the agency retained Dr. Jules Coleman, director of psychiatry at Yale University School of Medicine, to study the problem and recommend a solution. His chief recommendation was the disbanding of the Child Guidance Department and the establishment of a central psychiatric clinic under the direction of a well-qualified child psychiatrist.

Before Dr. Coleman's study was completed, however, the agency's greatly loved executive director, Louis Sobel, drowned when the excursion boat on which he was a passenger sank in Chesapeake Bay. In the years following the tragic death of the internationally recognized social work leader there were several changes in chief executive which delayed implementation of the Coleman recommendations.

At last, in 1960, associate executive director Esther Simon who had for the second time assumed the post of acting executive director, met with JCCA president Irving Mitchell Felt and Mrs. Ada Slawson, head of the agency's Child Guidance Committee to put the plan into motion.

September 1, 1961, the clinic was formally established with Dr. Leonard Hollander of Albert Einstein Medical College's Department of Psychiatry as its first director and Mrs. Slawson as chief psychiatric social worker. Twenty-one months later it was licensed by the New York State Department of Mental Hygiene.

By 1971, the staff of the JCCA psychiatric clinic included 11 psychiatrists and 8 psychologists, in addition to its present director, Dr. Sol Nichtern, former chief of adolescent psychiatric services at Hillside Hospital. The residential treatment centers had an additional 4 psychiatrists under Dr. Nichtern's direction. Since September, 1962, the agency also has had the services of a chief psychologist.

Gradually, psychiatric consultation was extended into the various units of the agency so that today all the major divisions have direct services within their own program. The clinic staff contributes to all phases of the agency's work. This includes consultation on intake, undercare and aftercare, staff training and research, as well as treatment and diagnostic consultation.

In 1971, the annual agency budget for psychiatric and psychological services reached the sum of $350,000. The overall agency allocation of psychiatric time: 360 hours weekly.

Growing cooperation with sister agencies led almost inevitably to further mergers. There were no fifes and drums but there should have been, that day in 1960 when the Brooklyn children formally returned to the Manhattan fold.

It was 82 years since the overcrowded HOA had "summarily abandoned the responsibility" for the care of Brooklyn children. The hurt feelings born of that abrupt rejection had been put aside in 1922 long enough for the Brooklyn board to present its Manhattan cousins with an embossed and framed resolution felicitating them on the completion of 100 years of child-caring work. This fine gesture prompted 15 members of the HOA board, headed by their president, to reciprocate by crossing the bridge to pay the Brooklyn institution their first visit in its 44 years of existence. "An unusual mark of attention" commented the gratified BHOA president.

But it was the extensive collaborative work of the fifties — after institutional rivalries and ancient hurts had long since given way to shared convictions and policies — that brought the two agencies closer and closer together. Their co-sponsorship of the Family Day Care program and of the Tri-Agency program led directly to the decision to merge. First, in 1958, they merged their intake and foster homefinding services and staff training. Finally, in May, 1960, they merged their total organizations.

With the merger, the Jewish Youth Services of Brooklyn brought in to JCAA 125 foster homes serving 200 Brooklyn Jewish children, an able staff, a headquarters building at 150 Court Street, and the Girls' Club of Brooklyn with its 30 young women residents. Several JYSB board members were elected JCCA trustees, and in time provided the agency with three presidents, including the present incumbent, Edward Elman.

That same year, JCCA took over intake service for the four group residences of Hartman-Homecrest, an orthodox children's agency. In 1962, the two agencies were consolidated and the Hartman-Homecrest facilities — serving 54 boys and girls — were added to JCCA's group residence division. By agreement, all four new facilities would retain their kosher kitchens. Another old mistrust had been dissolved in the common professional concern for better care for Jewish children and the shared wish for an unduplicated single service to which Jewish families might turn in time of need.

Hartman-Homecrest itself had been the product of an earlier merger of the two Orthodox institutions mentioned in Chapter IV. The Hebrew National Orphan Asylum, renamed "Homecrest" by its boys in 1947 to erase the resented and no longer accurate term "orphan asylum," and the Israel Orphan Asylum, renamed the Gustave Hartman Home for Children in honor of its founder, had joined forces in 1953.

Both Orthodox agencies had undergone sweeping changes since their early shift to the suburbs. The Hebrew National Orphan Asylum in 1922 had moved its 6 to 13 year old boys into a former Home for the Aged in Yonkers with 22 acres and room for 300 children. The Israel Orphan Asylum in 1923 had bought a large Victorian mansion in Far Rockaway to use as a summer home for its little boys and girls, ages 1 to 6; in 1944, the house was converted into a year-round residence. Later it had extended placement age to 14 for the girls only. Boys continued to be transferred at six to the HNOH.

After the merger in 1956, Reuben Koftoff, under whose long-term directorship the HNOH program had been drastically refashioned, was appointed director of the new agency. Hartman-Homecrest closed its two congregate orphanages, returned most of their children home — as so many had done before — or transferred them to the foster home facilities of JCCA and JYSB, and opened the attractive group residences that now in 1962 joined the JCCA group residence division. These included two agency-owned co-ed private houses for youngsters 7 to 15 — one caring for 22 youngsters on the site of the former Gustave Hartman Home, the other for 16 children in Mount Vernon. Another two agency-rented apartment residences in Howard Beach (Queens) later were transferred by JCCA to a new housing development in Rego Park. These care for eight teenagers each — one for boys, one for girls.

The consolidation of JCCA and Hartman-Homecrest signalled also the retirement as administrator of May Hartman, widow of Judge Hartman and, for almost half a century, one of New York's most extraordinarily gifted fund raisers. Her annual star-studded fund-raising affairs at Madison Square Garden, from 1921 to 1960 — organized almost single-handedly — had largely financed throughout most of its 39-year independent existence the operation of the home named after her husband. Mrs. Hartman, Samuel Field and six other H-H leaders joined the JCCA board. Koftoff and other staff members joined the JCCA Group Residence Division.

By agreement, part of the original Hartman-Homecrest land and approximately $1,000,000 in H-H funds were allocated to Federation for the construction of two needed community centers for Queens families — the Gustave Hartman YM-YWHA in Far Rockaway, and the Samuel Field YM-YWHA in Little Neck. The balance became part of the assets of the newly consolidated agency.

Another consolidation was yet to come. In July, 1970, Childville, a unique non-sectarian residential treatment center for severely emotionally disturbed young children, added its experienced staff and its 58 boys and girls to the JCCA's range of child care services. The children, from 6 to 14 years old, are cared for in an 8-story building on East 88th Street, remodelled in 1970 at a cost of $1,000,000, and in two small group homes in Flushing.

The Child Welfare League has described Childville as "one of the few voluntary agencies which accept children with 'psychotic process'" and has commended it for "its clinical courage in accepting the challenges and its clinical tenacity in its efforts on behalf of individual children."

The keystone of the unusual treatment program, developed by Childville's medical director, Morton P. Svigals, M.D., is the participation of the full staff — social work therapists, child care workers and teachers — in a therapeutic group process which, he explains, "facilitates free communication of attitudes and feelings and profoundly affects the child's environment and treatment." A Board of Education special public school — P.S. 368 — functions within the Childville residence.

Childville's present program represents a total metamorphosis since the day the agency opened its doors in 1916 as the Daughters of Zion Hebrew Day Nursery, serving Orthodox Jewish children in Williamsburg. Later, it enlarged its scope as the Children's Day and Night Shelter. In 1952, to meet an urgent community need, it transformed its service into a non-sectarian residential treatment center and, renamed Childville, adopted its present program. In 1970 it moved from outworn Brooklyn premises to its present site.

With its consolidation into the JCCA, Childville's president, Mrs. Salim Lewis, and four other trustees joined the enlarged agency's board.

JCCA's two oldest institutions, the Pleasantville Cottage School and the Edenwald School, also have undergone important changes since 1950. But the changes have involved no metamorphoses, but rather improvements on already basically sound and essential programs, and large-scale development and upgrading of physical facilities.

A major event to the 190 Pleasantville children was the fiery 1968 destruction of the main building, which had housed both offices and public school classrooms. It was a vivid and only moderately terrifying four-alarm conflagration, since happily no one was injured, and the youngsters, formed into a rescue brigade under two teachers, salvaged all of the venerable religious objects from the handsome synagogue on the top floor. A new and creatively planned modern school plant was built, and the main building was remodelled for use as a treatment and operations center, at a total combined cost of over $3,000,000. The new education building — which provides facilities for Union Free School District #4, Town of Mount Pleasant, serving the PCS children — opened in the fall of 1971. For the first time, the admission of 50 day students from Westchester now became possible. The 50 include ten severely disturbed children aged 9 to 12 enrolled in the Day Treatment and Educational Program launched the preceding year, and 40 in the new Day School Program. The Day Treatment Program represents another step in the agency's attempts to extend its therapeutic skills to larger numbers of troubled children and families while helping them avoid separation. The Day School Program makes the UFSD #4's special educational program available to Westchester children who, while less severely troubled, have emotional problems which make it impossible for them to successfully utilize a regular school program.

Edenwald today is a residential treatment center for 64 retarded boys and girls between 8 and 16, located on a property reduced to 17 acres by sales to the city and the Catholic Archbishopric of New York. But its program has grown.

In 1959, the school was the subject of a study by Dr. Jules Coleman, who previously had evaluated the JCCA's psychiatric services. Now the Yale University psychiatrist was asked to rule on the effectiveness of the Edenwald program and the appropriateness of a treatment center for the retarded in the constellation of JCCA services.

Dr. Coleman strongly affirmed the school's place among JCCA services. He pointed out that the reasons why the Edenwald children needed placement were no different from the reasons other JCCA young people needed the agency's help. They, too, came from disturbed families and their placement had come about not primarily because of the child's retardation but because the stresses and tensions caused by the interplay between family and child had led to an intolerable situation for all.

Dr. Coleman also found that, by and large, and "especially in the light of their psychosocial difficulties," the children were having "a favorable experience" at Edenwald. He recommended more effort to involve the children in the community and proposed small group residences for the older children to help achieve this.

Pursuing these recommendations, a small group residence for adolescent boys ready to leave Edenwald but unable to return to their own families, was opened in the West Bronx, in the fall of 1962. And Edenwald's program, under Herman Stern, has moved toward a greater emphasis on preparation for later work in the community. Particular attention is paid to behavior and attitudes on the job, always a difficult hurdle for the retarded. Half of the children are given work on the grounds to help them in their vocational training.

Most children attend the special on-campus public school, P.S. 612, and receive additional help from remedial specialists and speech therapists, as well as counseling, psychiatric, and psychological services. A few go on to junior high or high school in the community. Beginning at age 14, some children are given vocational testing and training through a special arrangement with the Federation Employment and Guidance Service. Older children get similar help through the state's Division of Vocational Rehabilitation.

All this steady growth in program, personnel and plant during the sixties obviously demanded further improvements in crucial central services.

In 1963, the JCCA and the Jewish Board of Guardians, a mental health agency for emotionally disturbed children, pooled intake for their various placement facilities in a "Joint Planning Service." In 1970, a study conducted by Dr. David Twain — former chief, Crime and Delinquency, Community Research and Services Branch of the National Institute for Mental Health — led to a drastic revision in general intake practices. As the present JPS director, Marie Laufer, explains it:

"Before 1970, we would see applicants ten times — sometimes over a period of 6 months — and try to make *more* than sure that they needed a particular type of placement while also preparing them for it. Now we try to telescope the process and quickly answer the question — 'to place or not to place — and where.' Because Dr. Twain's study showed that 99% of the children placed ended up where we originally thought they would!"

As a result in part of the emphasis on alternatives to placement, only 10% of the 4,616 inquiries in 1971 actually came into the two agencies' residential care. Others were referred to family agencies or to child guidance clinics (such as JBG's Madeleine Borg Child Guidance Institute); some to other placement or treatment facilities; and some were helped by short-term counseling at JPS.

The intake process now generally includes not more than one or two interviews over a period not longer than a month. The diagnostic tools have been considerably sharpened since 1945. Many applicants are screened out over the phone by a trained worker without further interview, and referred to other sources of assistance. For the others, case material is obtained where available — from school, the courts, other agencies. If needed, psychiatric and psychological diagnosis is provided by JCCA's Psychiatric Clinic. The material is then sent to the "undercare" facility selected for prompt consideration and action.

Equally broad have been the changes at the other end of the placement process — in aftercare. For many years, after the 1940 merger, aftercare was given little recognition.

The caseworkers felt it important to turn the child completely over to the family and the community. They were afraid to encourage prolonged dependency on the agency. "They so distrusted institutional ties!" recalls Sarah Sussman, who continued to head the barely recognized service.

Miss Sussman spent most of her time in liaison work with the alumni associations and in helping older alumni with counseling and modest loans or grants. Actual aftercare counseling of the younger people was expected to be handled by the undercare caseworkers — but little formal allocation of time for this was made.

In 1963, this situation — common incidentally to most child care agencies of the period — was corrected, and the JCCA became one of the first children's agencies in the country, according to Helen Rubenstein, to have a real "conscious, deliberate" aftercare program.

The new service, called the Post Placement Service and headed by Mrs. Rubenstein, was initiated in 1963 as a study and demonstration unit to attempt to answer several questions — and, hopefully, to implement the answers. What should be the scope of the JCCA's responsibility in providing aftercare service? What are the actual needs of the youngsters discharged from the different agency divisions? What supplementary services might an aftercare service require? The goal in every case was not simply to be supportive but to try for real rehabilitation and independence.

With a casework staff of seven, only children and families who could not get help through ordinary community channels were selected. Post Placement work proceeded with the older youngster and also with reunited families. In addition to counseling and sometimes psychiatric services provided, financial assistance may be given to meet special needs. This sometimes includes temporary support for a youngster — or phone bills, supper or fares for parents, who may need indulgent understanding before they can trust and cooperate with the agency. Employment agency fees, summer camp fees, tutoring fees, and supplementary allowances also may be provided.

Post-Placement represents a new phase in a youngster's progress toward health and maturity. The very fact of having a special after-care caseworker dramatizes a new surge toward future independence or return to family life. For many youngsters and also for families the post-placement period offers a real opportunity. The youngster faced for the first time with the need for self-maintenance, or the family faced at last with the day-to-day problem of coping with a returned child, recognize a greater need for help. Many, previously resistant, now are far more able to use counseling or therapy. Some youngsters have been helped to plan for post high school training; while others, with the added support of agency scholarships, have been helped to stay in college.

The nine year "experiment" has highlighted a number of important points. One is the lack of adequate resources in the community for helping young people. Another is the particular importance of continuing supportive service to youngsters with non-existent or fragile family ties — the youngsters who are "agency children." And, once again, the importance of starting work with parents as soon as possible to facilitate an early return of the child.

This principle, enunciated as early as 1919 by the then executive director of Fellowship House, Jacob Kepecs, is being tested, 51 years later, in the Special Emphasis on Early Return (SEER) project. Initiated in late 1970, the demonstration project hopes to prove that placement can be utilized as a phase in the treatment of a family rather than, as too often in the child placement field, a "career" for the child.

SEER currently is providing intensive casework and other services to the parents of four children in placement whose cases were selected at intake. The child and family have different caseworkers so that adequate time may be allowed, while staff and supervisors hold regular integration conferences. Foster parents or houseparents, too, are alerted to the plan for a child's early return home. The belief is that this service will significantly accelerate family reunion.

JCCA's three special services — Bi-Agency Project, Post-Placement and SEER — have proven costly because of the longtime, often intensive service involved, and, in some cases, the clients' need for financial assistance. It is an outlay the agency must carry alone, since there is no public reimbursement. But these services have spared many children and families the trauma of separation, or significantly speeded family rehabilitation and reunion. They have helped to reinforce and expand the gains made in placement, and to prevent renewed family breakdown. As costly as these services are in agency funds and staff time, they have in many cases saved the taxpayer the far greater cost of years of placement.

# Chapter 11

# Where Have All the Orphans Gone?

*"I want to tell you how much the French Jewish community, its leaders, its professional social workers have, during those last 25 years, been inspired and guided by the example of your Association, its programs, its achievements. We know what a unique task your Association has fulfilled, not only in the daily practice, but in the research field as well, and by spreading thus, far out of the United States new principles and methods in helping children and families with their problems . . . As your agencies have done, we also, over the years, have tried to go from child placement as an answer to all children's difficulties to preventive work with families. We too have abandoned the idea of large anonymous child care institutions for cottage-plan systems, off-campus group living, small treatment apartments for adolescents, foster home placements . . . We realize that the road ahead of us is still a long one and problems our agencies face daily are serious—staff is scarce and new difficulties arise in our Community with each new wave of refugees . . . More than ever, examples of Associations like your own who over 150 years have been able to adjust their programs to new needs, to new populations, in a changing society, will help us here to overcome present problems."* GUY DE ROTHSCHILD, PRESIDENT, FONDS SOCIAL JUIF UNIFIE IN LETTER TO JCCA ON ITS 150TH ANNIVERSARY.

EVERY year around Passover time, kindhearted citizens call JCCA offering to take an orphan for the holidays. It is hard to make the public understand that there are very few orphans today; that the Jewish orphanages—and indeed most of the others—have vanished; that most young children in care today live in family-like settings.

Yet many of JCCA's children are, in at least one sense, "orphans"—psychological orphans, robbed of their rightful homes not by death or destitution but by family break-up, or emotional conflicts usually born of the difficulties of their parents.

**151**

The number of children in placement today is, however, far smaller than in the past—and their ratio of the population is even more radically reduced. In 1904, out of a Jewish population of approximately 730,000, there were 3,000 Jewish children in New York City child care institutions, both Jewish and non-Jewish, or approximately .4% of the total Jewish population.

By December 31, 1971, with the Jewish population of Greater New York (since JCCA's area of service now includes Long Island and Westchester) estimated at 2,381,000—or more than three times the 1904 census—the total number of New York Jewish children in placement had dropped to less than half the 1904 figure. With some 850 Jewish children in JCCA residential care, approximately 240 Jewish children in residential care with the Jewish Board of Guardians, the other major Jewish agency offering residential treatment facilities; and another approximately 150 Jewish children in a few other small specialized facilities—the number in care today totals only 1240. This is .005% of the 1971 Jewish population, or *one-eighth* the percentage in care in 1904.

A similar drop in ratio, although usually not as steep, has taken place among other religious groups and in other cities.

What explains the dramatic plunge?

Principally, the broad social welfare programs enacted since the New Deal, longer parental life span due to public health advances, and increased community resources for families and children in need of help. And—for the Jewish community—the virtual cessation of immigration, and the greater stability and security of a settled population. Another factor is the recent decline in birth rate. New York State, in particular, the State's 1970 legalization of abortion and the widespread availability of effective contraceptives are sharply reducing the numbers of unwanted children.

Community resources like group day care and family day care, homemaker services, family service programs, child guidance clinics, treatment programs offer viable alternatives to placement although they still fall far short of the need.

Despite President Nixon's 1971 veto of the Child Development Bill, which would have provided federal day care funds on a broader basis than ever before, existing federal and state funding more than doubled the number of day care centers in New York State in 1971.

Another forward step in preventive services in 1971 was broadened application of New York State's Greenberg Law which since 1957 has enabled parents—with the help of State Subsidies—to place in specialized private schools children too disturbed for the public schools.

The gaps in service are still great—and there is a continuing struggle in a period of recession simply to hold the gains already made. Budget chopping threatens many already undernourished family services. Measures like the recently promulgated New York State eligibility requirements under Federal guidelines, limiting subsidized day care to welfare and poverty families, increase the odds against struggling young families with marginal incomes—shut out by the prohibitively heavy fees levied on those above the poverty line.

Yet, despite the setbacks, there is a mounting tide of concern for young children and for family security. In the long run, it seems inevitable that growing public recognition of the need—spurred in part by the rise of the woman's liberation movement—will lead to broader Federal funding for adequate day care services and, hopefully, to more adequate family subsidies.

Even the broad preventive measures to be hoped for in the foreseeable future do not, however, suggest an end to the need for community care of children.

For the most significant factors leading to placement today there are no programmed preventive solutions. JCCA's 1970 population survey showed mental illness and emotional disorders as major causes for placement. Of the children in care, 21% had been placed because of the mental illness of parents; 20.4% because of the child's own emotional problems. (Virtually all of the latter were in JCCA's residential treatment centers.) Children placed because of neglect or abuse represented 11%; those in placement because of divorce, separation or marital discord were 7.9%. For what were once the basic reasons for placement—parental death or long-term physical illness—the percentages were 5.2% and 2%, respectively.

Just who are the children in JCCA care today? First, they are increasingly emotionally disturbed or physically or mentally handicapped; second, all but a few are native-born. Third, they are no longer always Jewish. On December 31, 1971, in addition to the 850 Jewish children mentioned earlier, 245 children of other faiths were in the agency's care, reflecting a recent significant change in traditional JCCA policy.

Of the 245 non-Jewish children, 166 were black and Puerto Rican. The black youngsters were not the first of their race in the agency's history. JCCA for many years had had in its care a small number of black and interracial children who were Jewish —often the offspring of mixed marriages or extra-marital relationships.

In 1967, however, in response to the city's critical shortage of child care facilities, JCCA's Board voted to open all its placement divisions to children of all faiths.

The shortage of placement resources had brought a critical overcrowding of temporary city shelters and an urgent appeal for help from the city's Commissioner of Social Services. Convinced the time had come for JCCA to take on wider community responsibilities, the agency's executive director, Jacob L. Trobe, and its president, Harry Rothman, visited one of the shelters, Callagy Hall. The sight of hundreds of children—sleeping in halls and converted classrooms—some waiting out years in these crowded, drab "temporary" quarters—proved overpowering. The JCCA president—himself a self-made East Side boy and well acquainted with poverty—delivered a moving report to the agency's board which led to an immediate decision. While continuing to meet its primary commitment to Jewish children, JCCA in the future also would serve children of other faiths as vacancies permitted.

Some of the non-Jewish youngsters accepted since that time have been the children of the current in-migrant wave of southern black families—casualties of a dislocation well known to the turn-of-the-century New York Jew.

And quite as well known to the agency's director! For four years immediately following World War II, Jacob Trobe served as Chief of Mission for the American Joint Distribution Committee, first in Germany, then in Italy. While directing JDC rescue and relief programs in both countries, much of his work centered on the establishment of children's homes, maternity centers, family kibbutzim and other forms of family and child care service for the shattered survivors of the European Jewish communities.

Like the Jewish children in placement today, the children of other faiths tend to be the more emotionally troubled or otherwise handicapped of their ethnic group. Here, too, public aid programs and family services have held together those families best able to cope.

Some of these handicapped children are in a sense the product of medical progress. Born with serious biological impairments, they owe their lives to wonder drugs and other life-saving devices. A few generations ago, similar impairments would have condemned them to early death. Their survival, often with severe handicaps their own parents could not cope with, brought them into placement.

Social stresses and changes in family living patterns have also contributed to the higher incidence of emotional disturbance in parents and children. More homes today are fragmented by divorce. In 1970, divorce reached an all-time peak of 715,000—an increase of 12 percent over the preceding year. According to the National Center for Health Statistics, the 639,000 marriages terminated in this country in 1969 involved 840,000 children.

Illegitimacy, too, continues to be a factor in foster care placement. Despite the birth control pill and abortion, 17% of the children in JCCA today were born out of wedlock. A good many of these youngsters are ultimately surrendered for adoption. A change in this pattern may, however, be indicated; with changing sexual mores, more unwed white mothers are keeping their youngsters—or resorting to placement only as a temporary expedient.

Many more families have been broken by mental illness or by drug addiction or alcoholism. The mobility of today's population has been another factor—destroying as it has the traditional extended family and the sense of community.

The recent curtailment of New York State hospital funds is possibly another reason why more disturbed children are found at JCCA today. Mentally ill children now stay an average of six months in a state hospital, instead of two years or longer. Voluntary hospitals which previously cared for young people for periods up to one year now frequently discharge them after a single month. Result: voluntary placement agencies often are asked to care for youngsters who have barely emerged from acute mental illness.

JCCA accepts more of these than most agencies because it has treatment facilities geared to helping them. The proportion of youngsters admitted from mental hospitals to the agency's Youth Residence Center jumped from one in nine in 1969 to one in five in 1971.

The widespread drug epidemic is also reflected in the agency's caseload. One in ten of the children in JCCA placement has at least one addict parent. Of these children, 25% were born with withdrawal symptoms.

Many of the adolescents admitted from hospitals or referred by other agencies today have also experienced hard drugs. Recently, one JCCA facility accepted a 17-year-old girl who had been "mainlining". She had just completed two years in Blythedale Hospital, the result of an overdose that left her for many months blind and unable to walk.

Discouraging as the picture may seem, it is important to remember that in significant measure the grim statistics of the child placement population are, paradoxically, the proof of progress. Social welfare and public health advances have all but eliminated what were the major causes for placement in the hard old days— parental death or family destitution.

Thanks to the growing availability of community resources, we have moved toward the hoped-for goals. More and more children and families, even in homes reduced to single parenthood by death, marital breakup or long-term illness, are being enabled to stay together.

Full orphans, rare today, are usually adopted. So, often, are out-of-wedlock children. As a consequence, placement with JCCA (and other agencies with therapeutic services) is now more and more often for children of the most fragmented and damaged families, and for children whose emotional problems call for residential treatment.

It should be remembered, too, that the youngsters in placement today are a small fraction of the community's youth population. Nevertheless, the special needs of today's troubled children demand continuing innovations in agency programs. The Youth

Residence Center, for example, requires that any young person admitted "be able to attend school or work in the community." But some of the youngsters recently admitted from hospitals have periodic difficulties meeting this expectation. And there are other young people whose needs cannot be met by any existing JCCA service.

How does one serve the seven-year old schizophrenic boy— now functioning on a retarded level—child of a mother committed to a mental hospital for allowing her two youngest children to starve to death? Here is a child too sick and primitive for Pleasantville, too young for Edenwald, and, perhaps, too retarded for Childville. How does JCCA help him?

Yes, his case is an extreme. But there are children with traumas almost as severe in JCCA's care today who would hardly have been admitted thirty years ago. It was not because they did not then exist, but they represented a far smaller proportion of the children in need of placement, and the agency had only begun to develop resources to care for children so damaged.

The problems grow increasingly complex as time goes on. Yet, there are also some rewarding answers. Many troubled children are significantly helped by the agency's present programs and resources.

One of the JCCA's strengths, over the years has been its ability to provide total care to the children in placement. For most special needs there are special programs, special services. The service includes not only casework and round-the-clock care, but also psychological and educational testing, medical and dental care, psychiatric therapy, remedial services, vocational guidance, and scholarship, recreational and vacation funds.

In 1971, the agency awarded its 2,000th scholarship. That year it provided a total of 105 grants for higher education. These were not awarded as they were in the program's early years. Then they went to the most brilliant. Today, the most brilliant usually can get help from outside sources. Instead, JCCA now gears its program to helping every child with potential obtain a post-high school education. If necessary, that help includes tutoring and supportive therapeutic services. The results are at least partially reflected in the fact that—in comparison to the national average

which shows that about 50% of all college students drop out—
more than 80% of the recipients of JCCA scholarships complete
their college training or career preparation.

Doubtless in part as a result of the supportive services provided, it is even rarer for a child in JCCA foster care to drop out
of school. There also are fewer involved with drugs, and fewer
suicides than among other children in their community.

Thousands of the agency's "alumni"—who are its raison d'etre
and its final product—have gone on to outstandingly useful lives
in their community. The JCCA Board today includes a number
of alumni from an earlier time. Trustees Aaron Jacoby (HOA),
Henry Kalman (HSGS), Louis Posner (HSGH), and Arthur
Rauman (HOA)—as well as many previous JCCA trustees, now
dead or retired—have all achieved eminent positions in their
chosen fields.

A majority of the youngsters cared for by JCCA return home
to their own parents after an average stay of three years in placement.

But what of the children who cannot return home? As a
better job is done of finding alternatives to placement for more
and more children, more of those admitted come from homes to
which they cannot ever return.

Theirs are the hard-core parents—the chronically mentally ill,
the drug-addicted, the retarded or those for other reasons unable
to assume parental responsibility.

The children of these parents—if they are older children, or
too handicapped for adoption—become the "agency's children".
They have only JCCA to turn to. But many of the younger children are placed with foster parents who would be suitable adoptive parents, while the agency makes every effort to obtain a surrender for adoption.

One new factor helping to stimulate adoption of agency children has been the state's recently enacted subsidized adoption law.
This provides an annual grant for foster parents with limited
income who adopt their foster child.

Fifty-two children in JCCA foster homes have been adopted
in the past 30 months (beginning January, 1970)—of whom one-
quarter are on subsidized adoption. Many were in what is gen-

erally described as the "hard-to-place" category—handicapped children or interracial or black youngsters.

Most of these children were freed for adoption as a result of sensitive case work with the natural parents. But the agency has also gone to court to obtain a termination of parental rights when possible if this is judged to be in the child's best interest.

And here there arises a persistent dilemma. Our society and its way of viewing children have changed radically in the past 150 years. But there is an immense lag between knowledge and implementation.

Child care agencies are frequently criticized for losing sight of "thousands" of children on their caseloads who might be freed for adoption by adequate agency initiative, planning and action. What the public does not understand is that most children in foster care are not available for adoption, and that it is only for a small minority that adoption is a suitable plan. Most need foster care for varying periods of time.

In cases where the natural parent seeks to regain custody of a child in foster care or to revoke a surrender, the New York courts have stressed the rights of the natural parent and have placed a heavy burden on the opposing party to show that the parent is unfit to have custody of the child. It is frequently stated that the child's best interest is paramount, but the courts often seem to assume that it is in the best interest of a child to be brought up by his or her biological mother.*

There may also be difficulties in freeing a child for adoption in cases where the agency considers a termination of parental rights to be in the best interests of the child.

Parental rights may be terminated under New York law in a case of a "permanently neglected child". A child placed in the

---

\* "Divorce, child custody and adoption laws and regulations, while paying obsequious obeisance to the 'welfare of the child', are often—advertently or not—the means for playing out adult interests, the venting of adult anger, the serving of adult convenience, the fulfillment of adult desires. A serious commitment to children calls for a re-examination of the laws, statutes, ordinance rules and regulations governing marriage, divorce, custody, support, paternity, adoption, dependency, guardianship and property rights in order to bring some clarity and coherence to a confused and often contradictory whole and to ground these policies and procedures in the primacy of the child's interests."—The Rights of Children—An Unexplored Constituency—Mary Kohler, SOCIAL POLICY March-April, 1971.

care of an authorized agency, either in an institution or in a foster home, is considered to be permanently neglected if the parent has failed for a period of more than one year following the placement of such child substantially, continuously or repeatedly, to maintain contact with and plan for the future of a child, although physically and financially able to do so. Attempts are now being made to broaden the scope of this statute so as to make possible termination of parental rights in additional cases. It is to be noted that the statute does not cover the case of a parent who is physically unable to maintain contact with the child. Difficult problems have also arisen in cases where the natural parent is mentally ill and, therefore, unable to function as a parent.

"With the increasing proportion of young children of long-term mental patients and of the long-term drug-addicted in foster care, there are thorny questions to which the child welfare field, the law and the courts must seek humane solutions", JCCA head, Jacob L. Trobe, points out.

"Foster family care, just because it gives children, especially young children, the vital experience of growing up in a family, with family ties and attachments, creates, on occasion, painful dilemmas—hard questions underscored by recent court controversies involving our foster children.

Although the cases which wind up in court battles are relatively few, these—and some of the other conflicts which never reach the courts—have deeply painful consequences for the child."

Legally, the mother or father who returns to the community as a self-maintaining citizen after years—six, eight, ten—of non-function as a parent—may—if even a tenuous contact has been maintained—claim a child in foster care since babyhood, a child to whom she or he is essentially a stranger.

Such cases point up a poignant question.

For how many years is it reasonable to preserve parental rights to a child placed in infancy—reared in a family with which he has developed deep emotional ties, in the absence of any other real maternal presence?

How to reconcile parental rights with the child's emotional well-being? Perhaps the answer lies in a new view, a new definition —of the rights of the child and of the child's "best interest"—a redefinition which both the legal and the child welfare fields must take responsibility in helping to shape.

Should the agency, toward this end, use its resources for the training of young lawyers interested in the field of child welfare and children's rights?

Increasingly, voluntary agencies like JCCA are moving to assume a larger responsibility and a more influential role in forming public policy in the broad areas affecting children and families.

In the belief that child welfare leaders must assume this role, JCCA was a prime mover in 1967 in helping to organize New York's dozens of voluntary children's agencies into the Council of Voluntary Child Care Agencies.

Through the Council, the united voice of the private sector now is being raised to influence public policy both at administrative and legislative levels. Already, a joint planning body has been set up by the city so that leaders of the voluntary children's agencies now have begun to participate with the public agencies in planning for the City's children in need of care.

The Council's influence and support has led to an important new development in New York's child care picture—a centralized information bureau, cooperating with city and state agencies, to provide information on all city children needing placement and on available vacancies. The Child Welfare Information Service is scheduled to begin operation late in 1972.

The Council has done much to improve service by facilitating planning and easing bottlenecks that blocked action. Exchange of information also helps member agencies identify and move into areas of unmet need, as well as to upgrade services.

On the legislative front, both in City and State, the Council is proving an effective spokesman for the child welfare field. With recent widely publicized adoption and custody battles sharpening public and professional concern over deficiencies in the law, the Council is giving special effort to winning improvement in the concept and scope of state laws governing adoption, custody and transfer of parental rights. During the 1972 State legislative session, the Council's recommendation to the legislator introducing a bill mandating a 30-day deadline for revocation of a surrender for adoption led to incorporation in the bill (popularly known as the "Baby Lenore" act) of a concept of real significance to the field.

161

The law provides that in custody cases involving attempted revocation "the parent or parents who surrendered such child shall have no right to the custody of such child superior to that of the adoptive parents, notwithstanding that the parent or parents who surrendered the child are fit, competent and able to duly maintain, support and educate the child. . . . The custody of such child shall be awarded solely on the basis of the best interests of the child, and there shall be no presumption that such interest will be promoted by any particular custodial disposition."

While controversy not infrequently brings about needed reform, there is no controversy about the nature of the children who are likely to need community care tomorrow.

Recognizing that these children will be increasingly troubled and damaged youngsters, JCCA sees the responsibility of the contemporary child care agency as the development of new approaches and new services to meet the needs of handicapped children, and the continuing improvement of existing services and facilities to better meet the changing needs of a changing child population.

1972 has thus far brought three significant new JCCA developments toward these goals. One is a pilot project—a short-term apartment residence for young runaways 12 to 18 years old in cooperation with Jewish Family Service—the Y.E.S. (Youth Emergency Service) House in the East Village. An effort at early intervention before the youngsters are exploited or victimized by the area's tough street people, YES endeavors, through counselling and other supportive services, to help young runaways to return to their own families, or to guide them into an alternative plan which promises schooling, job training, employment and safety.

The second is expansion of day care services—part of an increasing effort to serve children in their own homes, while preserving families. In addition to Family Day Care Service (which continues its steady growth) and the Day Treatment and Day School Programs at Pleasantville, a new group afterschool day care program has been initiated in cooperation with the Flushing YM-YWHA in Queens as a pilot project with supporting casework service for young children of working mothers.

The third and most ambitious is the undertaking of a major redevelopment of the Edenwald School. Recognizing both the urgent need for additional residential treatment facilities for the City's retarded youngsters, and the inadequacy of Edenwald's near-50-year-old plant—too crowded to adequately house its expanding special services, inappropriate in sleeping quarters for today's more disturbed, often hyperactive children—the Association is planning to build a completely new Edenwald Center with almost double its present capacity (including children in projected day care), on JCCA's 176-acre property at Pleasantville in Westchester. The new Edenwald will incorporate contemporary thinking on facilities for the retarded, disturbed child—an innovative school building, attractive small-unit living quarters, a clinical services building, and recreational and physical education facilities. The new Center—scheduled for completion in 1974—is also planned to incorporate a day treatment program—and designed to make possible the admission of younger children (present admission age is eight) at some future time.

At the same time, a major step to complete the ongoing modernization of the Pleasantville Cottage School has been undertaken. The Cottage School's 15 children's cottages are to undergo a total interior reconstruction. Although they have served well, the cottages have seen 60 years of hard wear. More privacy for children and staff and an attractive modernization of layout and decor are planned. A completely remodelled infirmary is also projected.

The nine million dollar investment these plans represent is the most ambitious the JCCA has undertaken since its establishment in 1940. A commitment to the most deprived and troubled of the community's children won Board approval of this major project—an effort which will require the agency's first capital fundraising campaign, as a part of the Federation of Jewish Philanthropies Building Fund effort.

The two-pronged effort—to preserve families and prevent placement wherever this is feasible, and at the same time, to improve and expand services to the troubled and handicapped youngsters who need residential treatment—continues to be the agency's motivating force.

The Child Welfare League of America, summing up after a 1972 reaccreditation study of the Association, notes:

"The agency truly acts as a parental surrogate to all children coming into their program. It would be hard to find a more committed comparable service devoted to needs of children. . . .

"The change in the administration of the psychiatric system has made for close integration of all professional disciplines which, in turn, provides much stimulation for service improvement. Exciting new approaches are being used here. . . .

"The commitment to service to children of other faiths as vacancies permit has been a major step forward.

"The Jewish Child Care Association continues to provide considerable strength, leadership and direction to the entire field of child welfare. Their professional competence is substantiated through their constant search for better ways to achieve their objectives. Their willingness to chart unfamiliar ground is indeed commendable. They have chosen to dedicate themselves to a continuing pursuit of excellence."

# Child Care Services Merged into
# The Jewish Child Care Association of New York

1822   THE HEBREW ORPHAN ASYLUM
       (founded as the HEBREW BENEVOLENT
       SOCIETY) to aid the sick, needy, widowed and
       orphaned of New York's Jewish community.
       For nearly 40 years it functioned as a
       volunteer welfare agency.

1860   The Society opened the city's first Jewish
       orphanage on Lamartine Place (now West 29th
       Street) with thirty children.  Moved 3 years
       later to 77th Street and Third Avenue, acquiring
       additional buildings in the neighborhood to
       house increasing numbers of wards, and for
       vocational training.  Made final move in 1880
       to Amsterdam Avenue, between 138th and
       140th Streets.  There additions were made over
       a period of years to meet the growing need.  In
       its peak year, 1914, the number of its wards
       reached 1592.  The HOA opened EDENWALD
       SCHOOL, a pioneering facility for the retarded
       child, in 1925.  The orphanage doors were
       closed in 1941, following the merger forming
       the Jewish Child Care Association; children
       who could not return to their own families
       were placed in foster homes.

1878   BROOKLYN HEBREW ORPHAN ASYLUM,
       organized because the Hebrew Orphan Asylum,
       inundated by the needs of new waves of
       immigrants, had restricted its service to New
       York children only (Brooklyn then a separate
       city).  In June, 1939, it closed the doors of its
       large institution, and, renamed THE CHILDREN'S
       SERVICE BUREAU, became a foster home service.
       In 1948 the Bureau merged with the GIRLS
       CLUB OF BROOKLYN.  The combined agencies
       became the JEWISH YOUTH SERVICES OF
       BROOKLYN, which merged with the Jewish
       Child Care Association in 1960.

1879   HEBREW SHELTERING GUARDIAN
       SOCIETY, founded to serve destitute children,
       orphaned or not, since the Hebrew Orphan
       Asylum now limited services to the orphaned.
       Opened its first facility at 57th Street and
       First Avenue; five years later had five buildings

in the neighborhood.  In 1887 moved to 150th Street and Broadway.  In 1912 it established the PLEASANTVILLE COTTAGE SCHOOL, in Westchester, one of the first cottage-style orphanages, closing its Broadway institution. In 1914 HSGS opened FELLOWSHIP HOUSE as a separate agency to serve alumni who needed vocational guidance and counseling.  In 1918 it established the FOSTER HOME BUREAU to provide foster family care for young children, as a result of growing conviction that family life better for children's social and emotional development than congregate institutional living.

1895    HOME FOR HEBREW INFANTS, founded for the care of Jewish infants and children up to 6 years of age, for whom Jewish orphanages did not provide.  It closed in 1942 to merge with the Jewish Child Care Association, placing its children with foster families or returning them to their own families.

1914    HEBREW NATIONAL ORPHAN HOME, an Orthodox institution established on the Lower East Side to serve orphaned children of immigrants from Eastern Europe.  It served 6 to 13-year-old boys only.  In 1922 the home moved to Yonkers, increasing its capacity to 300, and was later renamed HOMECREST.  It merged with the Gustave Hartman Home for Children in 1956; the combined agency, HARTMAN-HOMECREST, closed their congregate institutions and opened attractive home-like group residences.

1916    DAUGHTERS OF ZION HEBREW DAY NURSERY, opened in the Williamsburg section of Brooklyn, subsequently renamed the CHILDREN'S DAY AND NIGHT SHELTER as the program changed to meet community need.  In 1952, reprogrammed and renamed CHILDVILLE, it became a non-sectarian residential treatment center for severely disturbed young children. In 1970 it moved to a newly remodelled building in Manhattan and consolidated with the Jewish Child Care Association.

1917    ISRAEL ORPHAN ASYLUM, opened on the Lower East Side to serve children from one to

six years. In 1944 the asylum moved to
Far Rockaway; six years later it was renamed
the GUSTAVE HARTMAN HOME FOR CHILDREN
for its founder. Over a period of years,
extended its service to girls up to age 14.
Following a merger with the Hebrew National
Orphan Home in 1957, HARTMAN-HOMECREST,
as the combined agency was named, developed
small group residences in Mount Vernon,
Far Rockaway and Queens to replace their
former large institutions. Consolidated with
Jewish Child Care Association in 1962.

1922     JEWISH CHILDREN'S CLEARING BUREAU
created to provide central coordination for
clearing and intake service for the Hebrew
Orphan Asylum, the Hebrew Sheltering
Guardian Society and the Hebrew Home for
Infants.

1925     GIRLS CLUB OF BROOKLYN, established
as a separate agency by the Brooklyn Hebrew
Orphan Asylum to house working girls of
limited means, many of them young women
who had been discharged from the BOHA at
age 16 with no family to whom they could
return.

1940     JEWISH CHILD CARE ASSOCIATION
OF NEW YORK formed through the merger
of the Hebrew Orphan Asylum, the Hebrew
Sheltering Guardian Society and its Foster
Home Bureau, the Jewish Children's Clearing
Bureau and Fellowship House.

Since then, the following have consolidated
with JCCA:

1942     Home for Hebrew Infants (see above under
date 1895)

1960     Jewish Youth Services of Brooklyn (formerly
BHOA) (see above under date 1878)

1962     Hartman-Homecrest (see above under dates
1914, 1917)

1970     Childville (see above under date 1916)

# BIBLIOGRAPHY

## General Sources

Historical
(New York City
and Jewish)

STILL, BAYRD — *Mirror for Gotham* —
N.Y., 1956

ELLIS, EDWARD COBB — *The Epic of New
York City* — N.Y. 1966

SCHOENER, ALLON (ed.) — *Portals to America:
The Lower East Side, 1870-1925* — N.Y., 1967

RISCHIN, MOSES — *The Promised City: New
York's Jews 1870-1914* — Cambridge, 1962

GRINSTEIN, HYMAN B. — *The Rise of the Jewish
Community of N.Y., 1654-1860* —
Philadelphia, 1947

BIRMINGHAM, STEPHEN — *Our Crowd:
The Great Jewish Families of N.Y.* —
N.Y., 1967

POSTEL, BERNARD and KOPPMAN, LIONEL —
*Jewish Landmarks in N.Y.: An Informal
History and Guide* — N.Y. 1914

SCHAPPES, MORRIS U. — *Documentary History
of the Jews in the U.S., 1654-1875* — N.Y. 1950

ROSKOLENKO, HARRY — *The Time That
Was Then: The Lower East Side, 1900-1913* —
*An Intimate Chronicle* — N.Y. 1971

Social Welfare
(History and
Theory)

SCHNEIDER, DAVID M. — *The History of Public
Welfare in New York State, 1609-1866* —
Chicago, 1938

SCHNEIDER, DAVID M. and DEUTSCH, ALBERT —
*The History of Public Welfare in New York
State, 1867-1940* — Chicago, 1941

LUNDBERG, EMMA OCTAVIA — *Unto the Least
of These: Social Services for Children* —
N.Y. 1947

ZEITZ, DOROTHY — *Child Welfare: Principles
and Methods* — N.Y. 1959

FINK, ARTHUR E. — *The Field of Social Work* —
N.Y. 1959

KADUSHIN, ALFRED — *Child Welfare Services* —
N.Y. 1965

BREMNER, ROBERT H. — *American
Philanthropy* — Chicago, 1960

CHAMBERS, CLARK A. — *Seedtime of Reform:
American Social Service and Social Action,
1918-1933* — Minneapolis, 1963

NATIONAL ASSOCIATION OF SOCIAL WORKERS —
*Encyclopedia of Social Work*, Vol. 15 —
N.Y., 1965

STEIN, HERMAN D. — "Jewish Social Work in the U.S. (1654-1954)" in *American Jewish Year Book*, Vol. 57 — N.Y. 1956

FEDERATION OF JEWISH PHILANTHROPIES OF N.Y. — *The Golden Heritage: A History of . . . from 1917 to 1967* — N.Y. 1969

## Jewish Population and Immigration

LISOFSKY, SIDNEY — "United States Immigration Policy" in *American Jewish Year Book* — N.Y. 1966

HOROWITZ, C. MORRIS and KAPLAN, LAWRENCE J. — *The Estimated Population of the New York Area, 1900-1975* — N.Y. 1959

Statistics furnished by Max Mazur, Consultant, Program & Rates Analysis Section, Bureau of Child Welfare, New York City Department of Social Services

## Hebrew Orphan Asylum and Predecessors

*Incorporation Acts and Resolutions Appertaining to the Hebrew Benevolent and Orphan Asylum Society of the City of New York, N.Y. 1879*

*Incorporation Certificate of German Benevolent Society, N.Y., 1848*

*The Hebrew Orphan Asylum of the City of New York, 1822-1922* — (HOA centennial history)

HEBREW ORPHAN ASYLUM OF THE CITY OF N.Y. — *Report of the 99th Annual Meeting and the Ceremonies Commemorating the Centennial Anniversary of the Founding of the . . . 1822-1922*

POSNER, PHILIP M. — *The Hebrew Orphan Asylum, City of New York, 1910-1920* — unpubl. term paper, 1966

SACK, HARRY — *A Historical Study of the HOA of the City of New York* — Unpubl. thesis, Grad. School for Jewish Social Work, N.Y., 1938

HEBREW BENEVOLENT SOCIETY — *Minutes, 1858-75*

HEBREW BENEVOLENT AND ORPHAN ASYLUM SOCIETY — *Minutes, May 2, 1875 to December 18, 1892*

HEBREW ORPHAN ASYLUM OF THE CITY OF NEW YORK — *Minutes, January 15, 1893 to February 2, 1909*

HOA COMMITTEE ON ADMISSIONS AND DISCHARGES — *Minutes, 1902-1910*

HEBREW ORPHAN ASYLUM — *Report of the 87th Annual Meeting of . . . and the Proceedings Celebrating the 50th Anniversary of the Opening of its First Building, 1860-1910*

HEBREW ORPHAN ASYLUM — *President's Report, March 20, 1928*

HEBREW BENEVOLENT AND ORPHAN ASYLUM
SOCIETY — *Public School Detention Book —
Conduct and Lessons, 1879-1884*

HOA, LITERARY SOCIETY OF THE — *The
Chronicle of the HOA,* Vol. 1, No. 2,
September, 1904 and Vol. 1, No. 3, October, 1904

HOA CORNERSTONE BOX, CONTENTS OF . . . 1883

HOA ADMISSIONS, April 3, 1860 to 1909

HOA OF NYC, ALUMNI OF — *Seligman Solomon
Society, Annual Journal,* 1887-1909

HOA ASSOCIATION, ALUMNI OF THE — *100th
Anniversary Celebration Sponsored by . . . ,*
October 15, 1960, N.Y.

HOA *Bulletin* — various issues

HOA *Rising Bell* — various issues

*Interviews:* Maurice Bernstein, Dr. Maurice
Hexter, Sally Melnick, Nathan Loewenstein,
Chester Rohrlich, Murray Sprung

Hebrew Sheltering
Guardian Society
and Pleasantville

HEBREW SHELTERING GUARDIAN SOCIETY —
*Annual Reports of . . . , 1880-1909* in 3 volumes

HSGS — *Annual Reports* — 1911-13, 1922,
1928-1938

HSGS — *Building Fund Record Book, 1901*

LITTLEFIELD, OSCAR — *The History of the
Hebrew Sheltering Guardian Society: with
particular emphasis on the institutional aspects of
its program* — Unpubl. MSS thesis, Graduate
School for Jewish Social Work, N.Y. 1940

LEWISOHN, ADOLPH — *Autobiography* —
unpubl.

*Who's Who in American Jewry, 1926*
(Samuel D. Levy)

SHARLITT, MICHAEL — *As I Remember: The
Home in My Heart* — privately published, 1959

OHMES, FRANCES — *Scarce and Desirable: An
Essay on Peter Smith* — unpubl. MA thesis,
Florida State Univ.

SCHERMAN, BERNARDINE KIELTY — *Girl from
Fitchburg,* N.Y. 1964

OBERNDORFF, C. P., M.D.; ORGEL, S. Z. M.D.;
GOLDMAN, JULIA — "Observations and Results
of Therapeusis of Problem Children in a
Dependency Institution", *American Journal of
Orthopsychiatry,* Vol. 6, No. 4, October, 1936

HSGS, ALUMNI ASSOCIATION — *Reunion-
Dinner Dance,* April 30, 1932

CROWS AND RAVENS — *HSGS Cavalcade,
1879-1940,* N.Y. 1940

CROWS AND RAVENS — *Bulletin,* various issues

*Interview:* Julia Goldman

| | |
|---|---|
| Brooklyn Hebrew Orphan Asylum and Girls Club | BROOKLYN HEBREW ORPHAN ASYLUM — *The Institution That Emptied Itself, 65th Annual Report of . . . 1944*<br><br>BHOA — *Annual Reports,* 1890, 1894-1901, 1903-09, 1916-20<br><br>BHOA — *Souvenir,* 1899<br><br>MINSKI, LOUIS L. — *To the Contributors and Supporters of the BHOA:* Report of . . . President, 1922<br><br>SCHMIDT, MOSES B. — *Mother and Father to 700,* Address by . . . President, BHOA, 1923-1926<br><br>BHOA, *Minutes of the Women's Auxiliary of . . .* 1922-36<br><br>BHOA, ALUMNI SOCIETY OF . . . — *BHOA Bulletin,* various issues<br><br>*Interviews:* Aaron L. Jacoby, Eve Rabinowitz, David Farber, Marie L. Laufer |
| Hebrew Infants Asylum (later Home for Hebrew Infants) | RIIS, JACOB A. — *How the Other Half Lives,* Dover, 1971<br><br>HEBREW INFANTS ASYLUM — *Incorporation Certificate, 1895*<br><br>HEBREW INFANTS ASYLUM — *Annual Reports,* 1896 to 1917<br><br>HEBREW INFANTS ASYLUM — *Minutes,* 1905<br><br>HEBREW INFANTS ASYLUM — *Directors, Minutes,* January 1932-May 1942<br><br>LOWREY, LAWSON G., M.D. — "Personality Distortion and Early Institutional Care", *American Journal of Orthopsychiatry,* July 1940<br><br>BENDER, LAURETTA, M.D., and YARNELL, HELEN, M.D., — "An Observation Nursery: A Study of 250 Children on the Psychiatric Division of Bellevue Hospital", *The American Journal of Psychiatry,* March, 1941<br><br>GOLDFARB, WILLIAM, M.D. — "Infant Rearing and Problem Behavior", *American Journal of Orthopsychiatry,* April, 1943<br><br>GOLDFARB, WILLIAM, M.D. — "Infant Rearing as a Factor in Foster Home Replacement" — AJO, 1944<br><br>GOLDFARB, WILLIAM, M.D. — "Emotional and Intellectual Consequences of Psychologic Deprivation in Infancy: A Revaluation", *Psychopathology of Childhood,* Grune and Stratton, 1955<br><br>*Interview:* Esther Simon (Mrs. Frank Banker) |

| | |
|---|---|
| Hartman-Homecrest (Hebrew National Orphan Home & Israel Orphan Asylum) | HARTMAN, MRS. GUSTAVE — *I Gave My Heart,* N.Y. 1960<br><br>JCCA — *Background Information on Hartman-Homecrest,* 1962<br><br>ALUMNI ASSOCIATION OF THE HNOH AND HARTMAN-HOMECREST — *The Alumnus.* Several issues. |
| Edenwald | SIMMONDS, LIONEL J. — *Edenwald: An Experiment in Education,* paper delivered at National Jewish Conference, 1929<br><br>COLEMAN, JULES V., M.D. — *A Study of the Children and the Services at the Edenwald School, JCCA,* Sept. 1959 |
| Childville | JCCA — *Consolidation of Childville,* News Release, August 11, 1970<br><br>JCCA — Article on Childville in JCCA NEWSLETTER, Vol. 1, No. 1, 1970 |
| Fellowship House and Aftercare | ULMAN, GENE (ed) — *Fellowship House: Pioneer in After-Care for HSGS* — historical survey, c. 1937<br><br>SELIGSBERG, SCHWEITZER, AND BORETZ — *Re Follow-up and After-care Work,* Recommendations drawn up by . . . c. 1917, paper<br><br>KEPECS, JACOB, Exec. Director — *Outlook and Prospectus of Fellowship House,* paper, May 1918<br><br>FELLOWSHIP HOUSE — *Annual Report, 1918-19*<br><br>KEPECS, JACOB — *Fellowship House: Report Read at a Board Meeting, November 9, 1921,* covering July 1919 to July 1921<br><br>FELLOWSHIP HOUSE — Annual Reports in *HSGS Annual Report* — 1922-39<br><br>SUSSMAN TROMMER, SARAH, Exec. Secy, Fellowship House — *The Return of the Child to the Community,* paper read at Cleveland Conference, 1926<br><br>SUSSMAN TROMMER, SARAH — *After Care Work,* address delivered at Child Welfare Conference, N.Y., May 20, 1925<br><br>SUSSMAN TROMMER, SARAH — *Social Casework — After the Discharge from the Institution,* paper read at National Jewish Conference at Lake Placid, June 1935<br><br>SUSSMAN TROMMER, SARAH — *Material presented to Herbert W. Haldenstein on Fellowship House Activities for Use in Relation to Merger, March 13, 1939* (including reports on Sylvan Stix Workshop, dramatics, etc.) |

"Report on Post-Placement Service, April, 1965", *Crows and Ravens Bulletin,* May, 1965

RUBENSTEIN, HELEN — "Aftercare–Who Cares?", *Child Welfare,* April 1967 (reprinted by JCCA)

RUBENSTEIN, HELEN — Proposed Project re Reducing Time of Placement, Minutes Prepared by . . ., November 12, 1970

*Interview:* Sarah Sussman Trommer

| | |
|---|---|
| Jewish Children's Clearing Bureau | JEWISH CHILDREN'S CLEARING BUREAU — *Minutes,* May 25, 1922 — October 1927 |

SELIGSBERG, ALICE L. — "Jewish Children's Clearing Bureau of New York", Proceedings of National Conference of Jewish Social Service, N.Y. 1923

JEWISH CHILDREN'S CLEARING BUREAU — *First Published Report, July, 1922 — January 1924,* N.Y. 1924

**Intake:** KIRBY, JOYCE — "The Intake Period in the Child Placement Process", *Journal of Jewish Communal Service,* Vol. 33, No. 3, Spring, 1957 (reprinted by JCCA)

**Foster Home Care** BORETZ, MARY — *Speeches and Papers* in JCCA Archives

*The Homefinder: A Publication for Foster Parents* — March 1922-1957 (many issues from thirties missing)

LAZAR, LUCILLE, *Report on Baby Project of Foster Home Bureau, 1929-1935,* unpubl.

LAZAR, LUCILLE, Letter to Charles Schottland, July 10, 1946

BUREAU OF JEWISH SOCIAL RESEARCH — *Jewish Communal Survey of Greater New York, Child Care Section: A Study of Children in Foster Homes,* April, 1928

HOME BUREAU — Annual Reports included in *HSGS Annual Report,* 1922 to 1939

RADINSKY, ELIZABETH K. — "Provisions for Care: Foster Family Care" in *Foster Care in Question: A National Reassessment by 21 Experts* — Child Welfare League of America, N.Y. 1970 (reprinted by JCCA)

*Interviews:* Lucille Lazar, Elizabeth K. Radinsky

**Merger, 1940** BLOCK, HERMAN W. — *To Merge or Not to Merge: The New York Jewish Child Care Situation,* Address, National Conference of Federation for the Support of Jewish Philanthropic Societies, Phila., January 28, 1937

*The Proposed Merger of Child Care Agencies Affiliated with the N.Y. Federation for the Support of Jewish Philanthropic Societies: Its Implication for the Community and the Dependent Child Population.* A summary statement of reports by 10 sub-committees, May 1937.

BORETZ, MARY E. — *Foster Home Bureau of the HSGS,* Report submitted October, 1939 to Herman W. Block, President

THE NEW YORK ASSOCIATION FOR JEWISH CHILDREN — *Report of Audit for the Six Months Ended June 30, 1940.*

Jewish Refugees From Hitler

WHITE, LYMAN CROMWELL — *300,000 New Americans,* N.Y. 1952

STEINFELD, PAUL — *Problems of Jewish Children Survivors of European Concentration Camps in American Foster Homes, A Preliminary Study of 46 Cases,* confidential unpublished thesis, N.Y. School of Social Work, 1947

JCCA Statistics from Comptrollers Office

*Interviews:* Sara Egelson, Marie L. Laufer

Adoption

HELLER, ELSIE L. — *The Development of a Limited Adoption Program Within the Structure of the Foster Home Bureau,* unpubl. June 20, 1941

FOSTER HOME DEPARTMENT, JCCA — *Adoption Manual, 1946*

WOLKOMIR, BELLE — "The Unadoptable Baby Achieves Adoption", *Bulletin of the Child Welfare League of America,* Vol. 26, No. 2, February 1947

KAHN, MARGARET — *Report on Adoption Program,* unpubl. February 10, 1953

*Interview:* Lucille Lazar

Agency-Owned Foster Homes and Group Residences

MILLER, CLARA — "The Agency-Owned Foster Home", *Child Welfare,* November, 1954 (reprinted by JCCA)

APPEL, YETTA — "Report on the Foster Home Residence Project" presented at National Conference of Jewish Communal Service, May 27, 1957

*Friendly Home for Girls of the HOA,* N.Y. 1926

RABINOW, IRVING — "Agency-Operated Group Homes", *Child Welfare,* October, 1964 (Reprinted by JCCA)

Articles in *Our Children* (Oct. 1958, Dec. 1959, Dec. 1961, Feb. 1962, June 1962, Spring 1964, Fall 1964)

| | |
|---|---|
| Family Day Care | RADINSKY, ELIZABETH K. AND GORDON, BERTEL — "Day Care Families and Foster Families" in *Daycare: An Expanding Resource for Children,* Child Welfare League of America, N.Y. 1965<br>*Family Day Care Service Kit* (various papers) |
| Psychiatric Clinic | COLEMAN, JULES V., M.D., — *Report of Survey of Psychiatric Services of the JCCA of N.Y.,* March 15, 1956 |
| Bi-Agency Project | KIRBY, JOYCE — "Preserving Family Ties: A Report of an Inter-Agency Project", *Child Welfare,* Nov. 1959 (reprinted by JCCA) |
| JCCA General | *Changing Concepts in Child Care,* Professional papers presented at the Conference of the Jewish Child Care Association of N.Y. held at the N.Y. Academy of Medicine, January 7, 1954<br><br>SIMON, ESTHER — "The Changing Face of Child Placement Facilities and its Reflection on Practice," *Journal of Jewish Communal Service,* Winter, 1960 (reprinted by JCCA)<br><br>ADLER, JACK — "Separation, A Crucial Issue in Foster Care", *Journal of Jewish Communal Service,* Summer, 1970 (reprinted by JCCA)<br><br>JCCA — *Our Children,* magazine published October, 1958 — Fall, 1964<br><br>FEDER, REGINA — Chronology of JCCA events and growth from Nov. 1939 to 1965 prepared by . . . (in JCCA library) |

# Index

*(Note: A glossary of abbreviations appears on page viii)*

# Index

*(Note: A glossary of abbreviations appears on page viii)*

# Index

*(Note: A glossary of abbreviations appears on page viii)*

# Index

*(Note: A glossary of abbreviations appears on page viii)*

# Index

*(Note: A glossary of abbreviations appears on page viii)*

# Index

*(Note: A glossary of abbreviations appears on page viii)*

# Index

*(Note: A glossary of abbreviations appears on page viii)*

# Index

*(Note: A glossary of abbreviations appears on page viii)*

# Index

*(Note: A glossary of abbreviations appears on page viii)*

# Index

*(Note: A glossary of abbreviations appears on page viii)*

**185**

# Index

*(Note: A glossary of abbreviations appears on page viii)*

Grateful acknowledgement is made to Robert Sorg and the Sorg Printing Corporation and to David Kosh and the Case Paper Corporation, whose generous donation of printing services and paper helped to make possible the production of THE CHILDREN YOU GAVE US. We are grateful also to Walter Harris and Harry Rothman for their generous grants and to our other trustees whose contributions to our Sesquicentennial Fund helped to meet other publication costs.

Cover and book design — Alan Peckolick
Editorial Consultant — Helene B. Weintraub